access to religion and philosophy

Medical Ethics

access to religion and philosophy

a
t
r
p

Medical Ethics

Michael Wilcockson

HODDER
EDUCATION
AN HACHETTE UK COMPANY

I am very grateful to Nicholas Leathers, Edward Russell and Robert Stewart for their comments and advice on many parts of this book. But I am especially indebted to Alison Wilcockson for her close critical reading of the whole book.

The Publishers would like to thank the following for permission to reproduce copyright material:

Photo credits

Cover © Christian Darkin/Science Photo Library, **p.6** © The Print Collector/Alamy; **p.27** © Najlah Feanny/Corbis; **p.51** © Larry Mulvehill/Corbis; **p.100** (left) © Pictorial Press Ltd/Alamy; **p.100** (right) © Content Mine International/Alamy; **p.123** © BBC; **p.133** Oregon Health and Science University

Acknowledgements

p.28 Penguin for the quote from *Dictionary of Philosophy* by Thomas Mautner (Penguin Books, 1997); **p.34** *Daily Telegraph* for the quote from 'Vicar loses court battle to prosecute doctors over abortions', by Sarah Womack, 17 March 2005; **p.34** *The Times* for the quote from 'Abortions soar as careers come first', by Alexandra Frean, 28 July 2005; **p.39** The Office of Public Sector Information (OPSI) for the abortion statistics published by Department of Health, Bulletin 2007/01. Reproduced under the terms of the Click-Use Licence; **pp.52–53** *The Times* for the quote from 'Cheers as GP is cleared of murdering patient; Trial', by Paul Wilkinson, 12 May 1999; **pp.65–66** McGraw Hill for the quote from *Classic Cases in Medical Ethics* by Gregory Pence (McGraw Hill, 2007); **p.86** *The Times* for the headline 'Designer baby fears over heart gene test approval', 15 December 2007; **p.90** Based on a diagram in 'Preimplantation of embryo development' from *Embryo Experimentation: ethical, legal and social issues*, Singer (ed.) *et al.*, 1990, CUP, p. 5

Every effort has been made to trace all copyright holders, but if any have been inadvertently overlooked the Publishers will be pleased to make the necessary arrangements at the first opportunity.

Although every effort has been made to ensure that website addresses are correct at time of going to press, Hodder Education cannot be held responsible for the content of any website mentioned in this book. It is sometimes possible to find a relocated web page by typing in the address of the home page for a website in the URL window of your browser.

Hachette's policy is to use papers that are natural, renewable and recyclable products and made from wood grown in sustainable forests. The logging and manufacturing processes are expected to conform to the environmental regulations of the country of origin.

Orders: please contact Bookpoint Ltd, 130 Milton Park, Abingdon, Oxon OX14 4SB. Telephone: +44 (0)1235 827720. Fax: +44 (0)1235 400454. Lines are open 9.00a.m.–5.00p.m., Monday to Saturday, with a 24-hour message answering service. Visit our website at www.hoddereducation.co.uk

© Michael Wilcockson 2008

First published in 2008
by Hodder Education,
an Hachette UK company
338 Euston Road
London NW1 3BH

Impression number   5 4

Year   2012

Illustrations by Alex Machin, Barking Dog Art and GreenGate Publishing Services
Typeset in Bembo by GreenGate Publishing Services, Tonbridge, Kent
Printed in India

A catalogue record for this title is available from the British Library

ISBN: 978 0340 95777 6

CONTENTS

PREFACE

To the student

Access books are written mainly for students studying for examinations at higher level, particularly GCE Advanced Subsidiary (AS) level and Advanced (A) level. A number of features have been included to assist students, such as the study guides at the end of chapters.

To use these books most effectively, you should be aware of the following features:

- At the beginning of each chapter there is a checklist, which is a brief introduction about the key elements that the chapter covers.
- Key questions, words, people, thoughts and quotes in the margin highlight specific points from the main text.
- Profiles of key individuals give information on a philosopher's background and work.
- There are summary diagrams throughout the chapters to aid revision.
- The revision checklist at the end of each chapter summarises the main points.

General advice on answering essay questions

Structured questions will tell you what to include. The following advice is for those questions which leave it to you to work out.

- The most important thing is to read the question carefully and work out what it really means. Make sure you understand all the words in the question (you may need to check some of them in the dictionary or look up technical terms in the glossary at the back of this book).
- Gather the relevant information for answering the question. You will probably not need everything you know on the topic. Keep to what the question is asking.
- Organise your material by drawing up a plan of paragraphs. Make sure that each paragraph is relevant to the question. Include different views within your answer (most questions require arguments for and against).

- Start with an introduction that explains in your own words what the question is asking and defines any technical words. Work through your answer in carefully planned paragraphs. Write a brief conclusion in which you sum up your answer to the question (without repeating everything in the essay).

Chapter checklist ✓

This chapter considers the relationship between professional doctors' ethics and general views of ethics. This poses many philosophical problems, notably whether doctors' ethics should be deontological (i.e. rule-based), consequential (i.e. situational) or virtue-based (i.e. character-based). In the past there have been many codes of ethics for doctors. What should a code contain today? Some suggest the four principles of autonomy, non-maleficence, beneficence and justice. Three other important issues are also considered: confidentiality and privacy; money and the distribution of resources; and the relationship of medical ethics and the law.

1 Doctors' ethics

Case study
A doctor's dilemma

A patient with chronic renal failure became more and more unhappy with measures taken to preserve his kidney function and his basic health. One night in a rage he pulled at the 'shunt' in his arm through which he was attached to the kidney machine, and infection resulted. His arm became gangrenous and he refused to allow anyone to operate. He insisted he wanted to die. The renal physician thought he was insane, and called in a psychiatrist. The psychiatrist did not agree, and considered him depressed but sane, and thought he had made a rational choice of death.

(Alastair V. Campbell and Roger Higgs, *In That Case*, 1982, page 16)

How should the doctor behave? Should he respect his patient's autonomy or should he do what he thinks is in the best interests of his patient? The case illustrates the difficulty balancing a doctor's professional ethics and respect for a patient's own morality.

Are there doctors' ethics? In many areas of modern life where people are involved in distinctive professions special forms of ethical codes have developed. **Professional ethics** therefore refers to the codes drawn up for teachers, lawyers, business people, health carers, police, etc. Professional ethics raises a number of basic questions:

- What is the relationship between professional ethics and society's ethics?
- On what philosophical basis are these ethics formed?
- What makes a particular professional ethic distinctive?

a) What are ethics?

To answer these questions we have to begin by asking what is meant by ethics.

- **Ethics** is the philosophical means of investigating the principles and theories of the moral life.

Ethics can be divided into the following.

- **Normative ethics** refers to a particular moral system of thought which has established what standards are right and wrong. For example, utilitarianism suggests that something is right insofar as it produces the greatest happiness for the greatest number.
- **Descriptive ethics** reports what people believe and how they behave. This might be investigated by anthropologists, sociologists or psychologists. Descriptive ethics might conclude that as people believe and do things very differently in different cultures that ethics are relative and not absolute.
- **Meta-ethics** is the philosophical process which looks at the meanings of words such as good, bad, right, wrong, justice, virtue, responsibility, etc. It considers whether these words have **objective** meaning, that is, whether they refer to distinctive abstract qualities in the world, or whether they have **subjective** meaning, that is, whether they refer to human ideas. Meta-ethics looks for consistency of terms and language.

These terms overlap considerably and in practice normative ethics and meta-ethics rely on each other a great deal, whilst descriptive ethics provides information by which meta-ethics develops its theories.

Key question

What should be the relationship between professional medical ethics and society's ethics?

b) Professional medical ethics and society's ethics

Professional ethics therefore has to go through the process of defining what is meant by good and bad within the narrower confines of a particular **practice**, and the **skills** and **knowledge** which are associated with it. The practice here is medicine.

Key question

What is the meta-ethical basis for medical ethics?

Key words

The principle of **sufficient reason** was developed by Leibnitz and states that for every fact there must be a reason why it is so.

Deontology in ethics is the belief that there are duties or rules that are intrinsically right.

Key thought

Hegel criticised Kant for developing empty formalism. For example if the rule is not to cause harm, is a doctor right or wrong to help someone to commit suicide if they are in pain? The rule by itself does not seem to be of much practical help.

Key word

An **infinite regress** is where each idea implies a preceding idea without an origin. If this is so there is no reason to accept any one idea as being any more authoritative than any other.

Key thought

Normative deontological systems might include natural law, Kantian ethics and revealed ethics (such as Christian, Islamic and Jewish ethics).

However, medical ethics do not exist in their own separate world and must in some way work within society's ethics.

In theory any agreed code could form the basis of doctors' ethics. The code could, for example, consider it wrong publicly to criticise another doctor or to have a relationship with a patient. But there are various problems with such a view.

- It suggests a very limited view of ethics. A doctor is not necessarily 'good' because he has satisfied all the conditions of the code.
- Codes might fail to satisfy the wider public and to take into account other values which patients, for example, consider to be important.

For example a doctor might consider that confidentiality is a primary professional value whereas social values consider harm to others to be more important. In other words professional medical ethics have to **develop** within wider accepted values.

Deciding what these wider values are is notoriously difficult and this adds another level of complication to the doctor–patient relationship. But in philosophical terms the solution lies in being able to give **sufficient reason** for a belief and its action.

The need for a clear philosophical basis for medical ethics is essential to **justify** practice. The starting point is therefore meta-ethical.

c) Three types of ethical approaches
i) Deontological approach

One possibility is to take a **deontological** approach. Deontological systems justify actions in terms of the rules. So, in medical ethics, whenever a case x conforms to rule x, rule x must be applied. From the rules a professional code can then develop its principles. However, the problem with this as with all deontological approaches is:

- it is not always clear to know whether a case x actually conforms to rule x or to another rule (or indeed both);
- there is a problem of **infinite regress**. If the principles are based on rules and the rules are derived from principles there is no means of determining what the **basic rules** are;
- this approach assumes one normative ethical theory. But there are a number of deontological normative systems which would require another reason or criterion to determine which normative system would be the right one. If society had a clear moral view point, such as Christian ethics or natural law, then this might not be a problem. But in a plural society where there

Cross-reference

For further explanation read Mel Thompson, *Ethical Theory*, Chapter 2.

Key word

Surrogacy is when a woman bears a child for another woman or couple. See Chapter 5.

Key thought

Normative consequential systems might include utilitarianism. There are many different types of utilitarianism. The forms which suggest that rules are necessary to achieve the greatest happiness usually see rules in provisional terms as guidelines.

Cross-reference

For further explanation read Mel Thompson, *Ethical Theory*, Chapter 2.

Key question

What qualities should the good doctor have?

Key word

Vices described by Aristotle are either deficient or excessive application of virtue. For example the vices of modesty are shyness and shamelessness.

Key quote

So virtue is a purposive disposition, lying in a mean that is relative to us and determined by a rational principle, and by that a prudent man would see to determine it.

ARISTOTLE, *ETHICS*, BOOK 2

are a variety of belief systems the deontological approach does not offer a sound basis for a professional code and perhaps resists having any set values at all.

ii) Consequential approach

Because of these problems another approach might be **consequential**. This approach often begins with existing practices and adapts them to new situations. It might do this by comparing like with like or by analogy. So for example when **surrogacy** was first being debated it was quite usual to compare it with adoption in order to establish its acceptability and the necessary medical guidelines.

However, the problems with the consequential approach are:

- it can lack consistency
- it has no sound established general principles on which to correct particular practices. The variety of utilitarianisms can cause confusion as to what the aim or end is. Is the aim the general good, the greatest happiness, the greatest lack of pain, the greatest preference, the most welfare, etc.?

The tension between deontological and consequential ethics illustrates the difficulty of establishing a code of practice for doctors.

iii) Virtues approach

Developing the virtues is one of the oldest ways of understanding the moral life. But it is only recently that professional ethicists have begun to rediscover their significance. Most virtue theories look back to **Aristotle** (384–322BC) as the one who most elegantly set out a virtue ethical theory. Importantly Aristotle considered that being virtuous or of good character could not be a private affair but had to be part of the **community** (Greek *polis*). In order to flourish (Greek *eudaimonia*) and be happy, people have to **learn** to do that which not only benefits themselves but others as well. By virtues or 'excellences' (Greek *arete*) Aristotle meant the qualities of character by which humans can live to the very best of their ability in a community. He distinguished between **intellectual virtues** which have to be taught and **moral virtues** which are acquired through upbringing and habit.

The most important intellectual virtue is prudence or *phronesis* (Greek), practical wisdom. *Phronesis* is able to judge in any situation whether a virtue is being pushed to an extreme in a way that is damaging to oneself and to others. It is the way in which the virtues can be actualised. Every virtue is accompanied by two **vices**. Virtue ethics therefore lends itself well to professions especially where care between people is of primary concern.

Key people

Tom Beauchamp and James Childress are two American writers who have written extensively on medical ethics. Their influential book *Principles of Biomedical Ethics* was first published in 1979 and has been revised many times.

Cross-reference

See pages 70–71 below to see how the principle-orientated approach might be applied to infertility.

Key people

Alasdair MacIntyre's *After Virtue* (1981) argued for a return to Aristotle's idea of virtue. This groundbreaking book has had enormous influence on modern ethics and is increasingly more significant for welfare professions who have felt that deontological and consequential ethics have failed to deal with the whole person.

Cross-reference

William F. May, 'The virtues in a professional setting', in K.W.M. Fulford *et al.*, *Medicine and Moral Reasoning* (CUP, 1994).

Key question

What principles should professional medical ethics be based on?

Today virtue ethics falls into two kinds:

- **Principle-orientated virtue** of the kind which **Tom Beauchamp** and **James Childress** suggest. Virtues correspond to principles and *add* to them. So, for example, the principle of beneficence correlates with the virtue of benevolence. To do this well requires practice and **skill** and involves other virtues such as **perseverance**, **humility** and **integrity**, qualities which may take a doctor or physician a life time of professional experience to acquire.
- **Virtue-orientated virtue** of the kind which **Alasdair MacIntyre** suggests. Virtues should be practised for their own sake. This is because virtues don't always correspond to a principle and it is important that virtues develop characteristics not just of the good doctor but the good citizen. In other words truth telling is not just a virtue for doctors but for all people in the community. Virtues should motivate us to do good things; virtues should not be subordinate to principles but develop what some have called a **cycle of virtue** within the profession but also for the wider society.

Importantly, as William May argues, the value of a virtue ethical approach to medical ethics is that it takes seriously the doctor–patient **relationship**. It reminds doctors that patients have feelings and moral principles which have to be taken into account. May argues that virtues are **performative**, that is, they don't just describe what should be done but actually add something new to society or a relationship. For example, a doctor who promises to see his patient next week isn't just making a statement of fact but expressing to the patient trust, reliability and genuine interest in his or her welfare.

d) Rules and principles

As was seen above, the tension between deontological and consequential ethics illustrates the difficulty of establishing a code of practice for doctors. For a code to work, there needs to be a relationship between principle and rules, changing situations and the development of medical science.

Beauchamp and Childress in *Principles of Biomedical Ethics* (pages 28–40) suggest that in developing a workable professional code for doctors and health care workers the following factors be taken into consideration.

- **Specifying principles.** As we have discussed, the strict application of rules/principles can be too blunt and fail to deal clearly and coherently with specific problems. Any code of professional doctors' ethics needs to be able to apply a rule to a specific situation.

- **Balancing and overriding rules.** There has to be a sound rational system where certain rules may be overridden by other rules. In other words actual obligations may legitimately replace **prima facie** obligations. Ross argued that this could be done by balancing one rule against another to see which one produced the greatest good. This is not easy. Appealing to the greatest good begs the question as to what this is. But in practice this is often the case and we judge the situation by what is the most appropriate duty in that particular case.

- **Four principles.** In the common practice of medical traditions four principles are often assumed. These are respect for **autonomy** (freedom to exercise one's will), **non-maleficence** (avoiding harm), **beneficence** (producing benefits) and **justice** (distributing benefits, risks and costs fairly).

- **Types of rules.** Rules are necessary in specifying principles to guide actions. However, not all rules work in the same way. **Substantive rules** are derived from the principles (e.g. rules about privacy and confidentiality); **authority rules** determine who may act and judge (e.g. who may override a patient's autonomy, who may decide on resources); and **procedural rules** determine processes (e.g. grievances, request for money and resources).

- **Rights, virtues and emotions.** The four principles have to be supplemented today by the rights of doctors and patients, the character or virtues of those who perform the actions (e.g. kind, courage, loving) and other moral emotions (i.e. a person's own moral values).

2 Conduct: confidentiality and privacy

Hippocrates (*c*.460–*c*.377BC)

The issue of confidentiality forms an important basis for many doctors' or physicians' professional codes of conduct.

For example the Hippocratic Oath states that:

Whatever I may see or learn about people in the course of my work or in my private life which should not be disclosed I will keep to myself and treat in complete confidence.

a) The importance of confidentiality

But why should confidentiality necessarily be so important for the doctor–patient relationship? The answer that many give is that it is based on a more fundamental right to **privacy**. But even here there is no agreed definition of what privacy is. Some argue that privacy is in some way linked to personal autonomy; that is, the ability to have self-control and self-determination of one's life. Others argue

Key question

Is the right to privacy a
fundamental right?

Key word

Instrumental value means that
an action is good by what it
achieves.

that autonomy and privacy are not interchangeable terms, rather
privacy describes the right for personal matters to remain personal.
In medical ethical terms, this means ensuring that medical
information when considered private must be protected from
unauthorised access by others. The right to privacy therefore also
has **instrumental value** in that it creates an atmosphere of trust for
relationships to work and flourish.

The last point suggests why, in such potentially sensitive issues as
health care and medical matters, in order for a doctor to do his job,
the respect for the right to privacy creates a relationship of trust
which a doctor needs in order to carry out his diagnosis.

However, if an instrumental view of privacy is taken it suggests
that there might be times when a doctor decides to override privacy
for more fundamental health care reasons. Privacy is therefore not
an absolute. This has important implications for establishing the
rules or guidelines for doctors when the right to privacy might be
overridden.

Confidentiality is when a person decides to give up some private
information to another in confidence. The recipient now is duty
bound to protect this information and may only divulge it to others
with the consent of the originator.

Cross-reference

Mark Siegler, 'Confidentiality in
Medicine – A Decrepit Concept.'
New England Journal of Medicine,
298 (1989): 1518–21.

But in practice the protection of confidentiality is widely
disregarded for the same reasons that privacy rights are sometimes
ignored. Mark Siegler, for example, considers that the easy access to
patients' records and private files in hospital to a large number of
officials has made confidentiality a **decrepit concept**.

The problem is where to draw the line. Consider the following:

- In an organisation such as a hospital it is a practical necessity for
  more than one person to have access to patients' confidential
  files.
- For research and teaching purposes case studies of actual patients
  are often used without asking for patient consent although the
  patient remains anonymous.
- Doctors often discuss their patients' health issues with other
  doctors.
- Doctors often discuss their patients' health issues with their
  wives/husbands.

b) Absolute ethical views of confidentiality

Cross-reference

For a full account of Kant's ethics
read Mel Thompson, *Ethical
Theory*, Chapter 10.

- **Kantian ethics**. The heart of Kantian ethics is based on the
  notion that a promise is a universal duty and can have no
  exceptions to it. A doctor who receives information from his
  patient is therefore assumed to be making a promise. Kant argues
  that it would be inconsistent and irrational to make a promise
  also intending that one might break it in favour of something

Key quote 99

Healthcare professionals have a right to disclose confidential information in circumstances in which a person is not, all things considered, entitled to the confidence.

BEAUCHAMP AND CHILDRESS, *PRINCIPLES OF BIOMEDICAL ETHICS*, PAGE 424

else. The attractiveness of Kant's position is that it firmly establishes the trust and **fidelity** necessary for the doctor–patient relationship to work.

- But there could be very good reasons why the absoluteness of the promise would be seen to contradict the state of affairs Kant has in mind. For example a doctor also has duties to protect the weak and innocent. If a patient told him that he intended to molest a child or murder a colleague at work then he might feel that these weightier rules justify breaking the ordinary rules of confidentiality.

- Beauchamp and Childress take this view and argue that duties are not absolute but **prima facie**. But they also agree that the place of fidelity in modern medicine has become weakened and needs to be reinforced.

c) Subjective and relativist ethical views of confidentiality

For those who reject an absolutist position but also acknowledge that rules are necessary as professional guidelines the following arguments might be used:

- **Utilitarians and consequentialists**. Confidentiality is necessary in order for a patient to tell the doctor their symptoms as fully and openly as possible. A doctor therefore should not divulge this information unless it has serious consequences for others. For example doctors should protect information about a patient who is HIV positive from his employers, insurance companies, even family. On the other hand he might choose to break the confidence if such knowledge would protect others, such as his wife or girlfriend, from being directly harmed.

- But the problem, as always with consequential systems, is how strong to make the rules. For example should a partner be told that their husband or wife has AIDS if the AIDS sufferer themself refuses to pass this information on?

d) Virtue ethical views of confidentiality

Beauchamp and Childress feel that fidelity has become weakened in modern medicine. But Kant's ethics are less concerned with people than principle and the utilitarian approach only values fidelity if it makes life easier for the doctor and possibly the patient. Virtue ethicists on the other hand suggest that the failure (if it is so) or the dilemmas caused by deontological and consequential approaches are resolved by rethinking medicine, in old fashioned terms, as a vocation.

William May (*Medicine and Moral Reasoning*, page 86) argues that confidentiality will depend on situation but it is equally a principle which is valued by doctors and society as a whole. The resolution depends on the key notion of Aristotelian ethics which is **phronesis**, the practical skill of striking the middle path between extremes. May commends the skills or 'marks' which the medieval philosophers suggested are needed to act prudently or wisely.

- **memoria**: being true to the past, what was said, what was promised
- **docility**: being open to the present, knowing when to listen or when to be silent
- **solertia**: being ready for the unexpected.

These 'marks' require other virtues such as integrity, humility, benevolence and justice so that confidentiality is not to be thought of in terms of rules or what is useful (for the doctor) but as relationship.

But for many virtue ethics fails to offer sufficient guidance especially in busy lives. MacIntyre's version of virtues is often considered too idealistic and depends on the almost impossible task of being able to determine what virtues society really does value. For these reasons virtue ethics has failed to make the impact on modern professional ethics which might have been hoped for.

3 Resources

There is no health or welfare system in the world which has infinite resources. The question of who should be given what and whose condition is considered to be more worthy than another is part of the everyday life of doctors and the health services.

Key question

How is the quality of a person's life to be calculated against a finite budget?

a) Quality of life in terms of a budget

The effectiveness of medicine has to be viewed in several different ways. Some medicine might improve the quality of someone's everyday life but make no difference to their length of life whereas other medicine might add significantly to their life years. For example a hip replacement certainly makes a great deal of difference to a person's mobility and their general enjoyment of life, but drugs and a machine which deal with kidney failure will keep a person alive who would otherwise die. But the distinction is not easy to make. Lastly, some treatments provide neither immediate improvement to the quality of life nor added life years but are given as preventatives. The early detection of breast cancer, for example, can ensure a non-life-threatening condition being treated before it becomes fatal.

The key issue here is one of the fair **distribution** of resources. Some form of calculus is necessary to consider whether, for example,

Cross-references

For a more detailed account of Bentham's utilitarianism, read Mel Thompson, *Ethical Theory*, Chapter 9.

Bentham's calculus can be found in Jeremy Bentham, *An Introduction to the Principles of Morals and Legislation*.

giving an expensive drug to an old but dying person is as worthwhile as giving treatment to two younger people who are not suffering from a life-threatening condition. The obvious moral system which appears designed to deal with these practical issues is the **act utilitarianism** developed by **Jeremy Bentham** (1748–1832). Bentham's material view of happiness does not make judgements about the quality of a person's life in any abstract sense but whether happiness (and the absence of pain) is likely or unlikely, short term or long term. His **calculus** therefore acts as a very useful check list for determining who the more or less worthy cases are:

- the quantity of pleasure against pain according to how **intense** it would be, how **long** it would last for (**duration**), how **certain** it was, how **soon** it might be encountered (**propinquity**);
- its *tendency* or effects, that is, how much **more** pleasure/pain would be generated (**fecundity**) or might it have *opposite* effects (**purity**);
- how **many people** it would affect (**number**).

However, in practice life is not so easy. Even if it makes more sense to treat the two younger people with the resources available, it would mean taking a decision *not* to treat the dying person and effectively allowing them to die. Perhaps we have to be less sentimental and accept that this is the harsh reality, but the public expect doctors to save lives, and to allow someone to die simply because the resources have been diverted elsewhere is not a principle that many would take if it personally affected them.

Tony Hope (*Medical Ethics*, Chapter 3) is one of the few who has argued for a more consistent Benthamite approach to medical resources. Hope gives the following example of three types of medical intervention and their benefits:

Intervention 1	*benefits 10 people*	*total life years gained: 35*
Intervention 2	*benefits 15 people*	*total life years gained: 30*
Intervention 3	*benefits 2 people*	*total life years gained: 16*

Which one, based on utilitarianism, should be followed? In Intervention 1 each person can expect an average of 3.5 added years, whereas in Intervention 2 each could enjoy 2 years and in Intervention 3 each could average 8 added years. Intervention 1 looks good value for money in terms of total fecundity but Intervention 2 would affect a greater number of people, whereas Intervention 3 succeeds in terms of duration. Hope argues that Intervention 1 offers the maximal benefit but:

> *In being generally happy with using resources to maximize total number of life years I am in a minority – and no health care system in the world behaves remotely in this way.*

(*Medical Ethics*, page 31)

The reason why the maximal Intervention 1 type acts are not performed is due, Hope argues, to a principle known as the **rule of rescue**.

b) The rule of rescue

The rule of rescue is applied where there is a person of high risk but who stands a good chance of success. The problem with Intervention 1 type cases is that, although some people may benefit more than the average, many statistically might benefit only minimally, whereas in Intervention 3 cases there is more certainty of benefits to particular people. The rule of rescue therefore makes a distinction between statistical people (people who might benefit, but are as yet anonymous) and non–statistical identified people.

So for example most health services would prefer to spend a lot of money (e.g. £50,000) on a particular person where there are clear and immediate life year benefits (for example on a kidney dialysis) rather than distributing a cheap drug to many people to reduce the likelihood of blood pressure but which will certainly benefit only a few people (costing for example £20,000 each).

The success of the rule of rescue is that it works by seeing actual results for a specific person, whereas statistical results remain less certain and are emotionally less satisfying and convincing.

Hope illustrates his argument against the rule of rescue with the thought exercise of a trapped miner. In this example it is the risks or the *costs* to the rescuers which has to be calculated. For example:

> *the chance of death for 100 rescuers is 1:1000 (i.e. 0.1 of a life)*
> *the chance of death for 1,000 rescuers is 1:2,000 (i.e. 0.5 of a life)*
> *the chance of death for 100,000 rescuers is 1:10,000 (i.e. 10 lives)*

So, the larger the size of the rescue party the smaller the risk of death faced by any one individual rescuer, but the trade off is that there will be more rescuers who will die in the rescue for the sake of only one life. The paradox is that certainty comes at an unacceptable cost. In other words it makes more sense to be one of a small band of rescuers, even though the risks are higher because the benefits are the same. The thought exercise illustrates that treating statistical people may be more risky in terms of knowing exactly who benefits, but it is more cost-effective.

However, Hope realises that there is great attraction in dealing with known people, just as the Australian government mounted a huge and costly rescue to save Tony Bullimore (the yachtsman who capsized trying to sail round the world in 1997). However, his thought exercise of the trapped miner serves to remind us that statistical people are still people and that health care distribution of resources must always bear this in mind:

The answer, I think, is not that we should become stone-hearted logicians and refuse to attempt the rescue of Bullimore or provide for renal dialysis. It is right that our moral imagination and our human sympathy are awakened. What we should learn from the logic of the case of the trapped miner is that our moral indignation must also be awake to the sadness of lives cut short, relatives bereaved, because we did not provide treatment for moderately raised cholesterol. Deaths are not less significant because we cannot put a face or a name to the person whose life could have been saved.

(Tony Hope, *Medical Ethics*, page 41)

4 Medical ethics and the law

Key question

Should law be independent from morality?

Key quote

But the law is not, and cannot be, an expression of moral feeling. It must apply to everyone, whatever their feelings: it must be intelligible and enforceable.

MARY WARNOCK,
A QUESTION OF LIFE, PAGE X

In many people's minds law defines what is and what is not morally permissible. In her introduction to *The Warnock Report on Human Fertilisation and Embryology* (1984) Mary Warnock makes it quite clear that law and morality are two separate matters. The aims of law today, she argues, are not to tell us what to believe but rather to protect citizens from harm and exploitation and to enable each person the opportunity to maximise their freedoms. But many would argue that such a sharp distinction in sensitive personal issues such as sexual behaviour and medicine is not possible.

For example the law in the UK presently treats euthanasia as a criminal act. Those who favour the law usually do so on the grounds that it is not for doctors or anyone else to dispose of any human life. This appears to be a moral value judgement and one which through common law tradition must be preserved. Some argue that such a law is an unnecessary infringement of human freedom and should at the very least be modified if not abolished. It is unclear whether the second view is or is not a moral value judgement. Freedom is treated by many as the necessary means by which to make one's own value judgements. On the other hand freedom is valued for its own sake because without it moral responsibility would make no sense.

a) The Devlin–Hart debate

The argument that certain kinds of private acts do cause moral harm to society was famously set out between the law lord **Lord Devlin** and the legal philosopher **H.L.A. Hart** over the issue of homosexuality in 1968. Devlin argued that law and morality cannot be separated. Hart distinguished between two moral problems. One is a **primary problem** which is whether an act is morally right or wrong. The second is the **critical problem** that if the law intervened in this matter would it be an unnecessary infringement of personal freedom?

Devlin argued the following:

- All private morality has an effect on the public morality. Public morality is necessary to keep society together and happy.
- Toleration of certain private acts does not necessarily have beneficial effects on society. For example just as treason is regarded as an attack on society, so by analogy is deliberate lack of morality.
- Lack of morality can be judged by whatever the general public considers in *strong terms* to be offensive.
- Whatever the public finds strongly offensive is **sufficient reason** to outlaw certain private behaviour to protect public decency.

Hart criticised Devlin's views for the following reasons:

- It is not obvious that private acts do have a *direct* effect on public morality.
- Does the analogy of treason work? Treason intentionally desires to undermine society, but this is not true in many cases (such as euthanasia or surrogacy, for example). The onus would have to be on Devlin and others to show that a particular act does create a climate whereby people abandon their ordinary moral beliefs, for example, that allowing euthanasia would increase murder rates.
- It is not clear what constitutes a public moral consensus and whether any reasonable person would necessarily know how everyone else in society feels.
- Even if public consensus could be achieved, would it necessarily have a rational basis? Many for example consider that capital punishment should be brought back, but such a view is considered by legislators and governments to be based more on emotion than sound reason.

b) Positive law

J.S. Mill's essay *On Liberty* (1859) is often cited as an example of the way in which law should function in a liberal society.

- The principle is that law is *not in itself* a moral guideline. Law in a liberal society acknowledges that each person has his or her own preferences which, using the utilitarian principle, if satisfied lead to the greatest happiness. The law enables the greatest personal autonomy of the greatest number.
- The second function of law is to **protect** the individual. This limits the majority from exploiting the minority and also the minority from exercising too much sway over the majority. Law should have minimal interference.

c) Moral dilemmas and law

Medical ethics and professional doctors' ethics have to take law into account. If Warnock is right a doctor cannot exercise his or her own moral feelings because the law 'must apply to everyone, whatever their feelings'. But in practice in difficult circumstances doctors find there is a tension between law and their own professional moral judgements. Euthanasia as we shall see is one such area of dispute but a more complex area is that of medical research and in particular embryo experimentation, gene therapy and organ transplantation.

Cross-references

Read Chapter 3 and Michael Wilcockson, *Issues of Life and Death*, Chapter 4 on euthanasia.

Read Chapters 5 and 6 on medical research.

Summary diagram

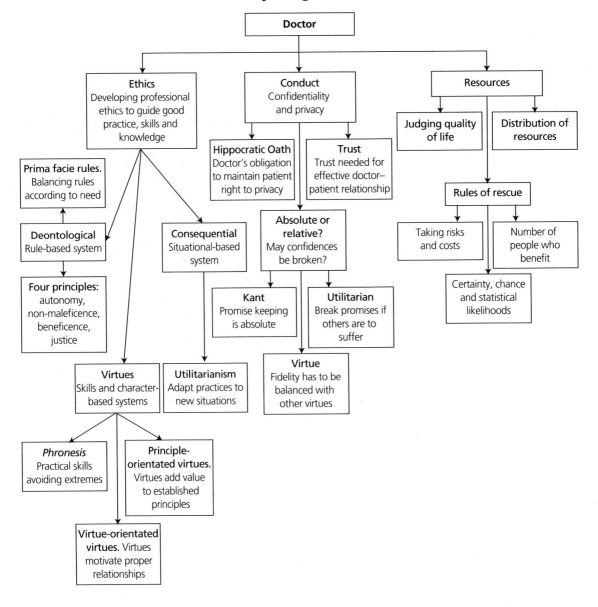

Study guide

By the end of this chapter you should understand what is meant by doctor's professional ethics and be able to explain how these ethics are formed. You should be able to discuss the differences between a consequential and deontological approach to ethics and the special place in which virtue ethics now has a place in modern medical ethics. Finally you should be able to consider the practical problems of patient confidentiality, the use and distribution of resources and the place of law in medical decisions.

Revision checklist

Can you explain what is meant by:

- sufficient reason in an argument
- virtue ethics and why they are important in modern medical practice
- why Kant considered promise keeping to be absolute
- 'life years gained'
- the 'rule of rescue'
- prima facie duties.

Do you know the difference between:

- ethics, normative ethics and professional ethics
- positive and natural law
- a deontological, consequential and virtue approach to ethics and to medical ethics
- the problems of distributing medical resources.

Can you give arguments for and against:

- using utilitarianism as the best ethical system to solve the problem of distribution of resources
- doctors always keeping patient confidentiality
- a doctor breaking the law on the grounds of conscience.

Essay question

AO1

Knowledge and understanding assessment objective.

AO2

Evaluation assessment objective.

1. 'The sole purpose of law in medical ethics is to protect people from harm.' Discuss.

It is important to be able to give examples of medical situations where harm is a particular issue. It might be an obvious example such as abortion or more subtle situations such as harm caused by loss of confidentiality. These examples need to be discussed carefully to show what kind of harm might be caused, and whether it is physical or mental. The next area then to consider is the doctor's professional code of conduct, in particular the relationship of autonomy, non-maleficence, beneficence and justice.

The question depends on whether the principles are to be considered within a deontological or consequential system of thought. The evaluative aspect might focus on whether a deontologist is absolute (such as Kantian or natural law thinker), in which case the deliberate causing of harm is always wrong, or weaker (as in Ross' prima facie rule-based system), in which case the rule not to cause harm may sometimes be broken because it might cause an injustice. The consequentialist might argue that avoiding harm is unrealistic and it is often a necessary means to an end.

Further essay questions

2a   Explain the difference between the consequential and deontological approach to ethics.

2b   'Rights are more important than rules in medical practice.' Discuss.

3a   Explain a Kantian approach to doctor–patient confidentiality.

3b   'There are times when it would be right to break patient confidentiality.' Discuss.

4   Assess the view that utilitarianism offers the best approach to the use of medical resources.

2 PERSONHOOD AND THE VALUE OF LIFE

Chapter checklist

Many medical issues are about how we treat persons. This chapter considers what it means to call a human being a person. Some consider a person is someone who has consciousness, memory and rationality. Others argue for an enduring self or soul which is given at conception or is potential from conception or develops later. Being a person determines how a life is treated morally. Two views of the value of human life are compared: the sanctity of life (life is intrinsically valuable) and quality of life (life is extrinsically valuable).

1 What is a person?

Case study
The ship of Theseus

Over a period of years, in the course of maintenance a ship has its planks replaced one by one – call this ship A. However, the old planks are retained and themselves reconstituted into a ship – call this ship B. At the end of this process there are two ships. Which one is the original ship of Theseus?

(Michael Clarke, *Paradoxes A–Z*, page 184)

> In the same way, over a life time the body replaces its cells many times over. So the question is, am I the same person as I was seven, fourteen, twenty-eight etc. years ago? And if, as in the ship of Theseus, those discarded cells could be used to reconstruct another replica body would it also be me?

Medical ethics is primarily concerned with the health care of people. By people we are assuming that this refers to all human beings. But this need not necessarily be the case. Other life forms may satisfy the conditions of being considered persons and conversely even a living human being may not fulfil all necessary conditions to be an actual person. Given that we often give higher priority to persons than merely living beings it is important to establish exactly what we mean by 'person' and therefore who is and who is not entitled to personhood.

a) Necessary and sufficient conditions

Let us suppose that each one of us knows that we are a person. What characteristics would this include? We might start by saying that I have to exist physically and this means being a member of *homo sapiens*. We might go on to say that I have to have experiences, emotions, show response to external stimuli, be able to communicate, have plans and be able to form a view of the world.

Now we might agree that each of these is a necessary element of being a person but that without consciousness personhood would not be possible. This might be expressed in the following way:

An entity is a person if and only if it is conscious.

This is known as a **biconditional** because not only is consciousness a necessary condition in itself but without it all other conditions would not be possible.

Consciousness

An influential thinker in modern debates about personhood is **John Locke.** Here is Locke's famous definition of a person:

we must remember what a person stands for; which I think, is a thinking intelligent being, that has reason and reflection, and can consider itself, the same thinking thing, in different times and places; which it does only by that consciousness which is inseparable from thinking and seems to me essential to it; it being impossible for any one to perceive without perceiving that he does perceive.

(*An Essay Concerning Human Understanding* Book II, Chapter 27)

Key quote

A human being is *'An individual substance with a rational nature.'*
BOETHIUS (C.512BC), *CONTRA EUTYCHEN 5 IN THEOLOGICAL TRACTATES*, 101–102

Key word

If and only if... statements are the usual way of expressing necessary and sufficient conditions.

Key people

John Locke (1632–1704) was one of the great English philosophers. His philosophy was influenced by his practical study of medicine and chemistry. He was influenced by Descartes but critical of his views. His book *An Essay Concerning Human Understanding* (1690) investigates the origins and limits of reason.

A person is therefore someone who is not only able to have conscious and rational thought, but also able to *remember* himself doing so 'in different times and places'.

b) Change and continuity

Key question

If a person forgets her earlier life is she now a different person?

The major criticism of Locke's proposal is the problem of **continuity**. Locke argued that just as the body changes and its cells are replaced or not replaced many times over in a life time, so may consciousness change. The question is whether these changes mean that we are still talking about the same person. For example, consider another paradox similar to the ship of Theseus given at the start of this chapter. If the members of a string quartet gradually change over ten years so that at the end of ten years none of the members are the same as the original four, could they still be regarded as the same quartet? We might argue that as each member was changed with another the others carried on the memory of the others so that although change takes place the string quartet still produces its characteristic sound (possibly improved or worsened by each new player). So Locke argues:

- Even if consciousness changes, a person retains their identity through a set of historical circumstances which are unique to that body.
- Even if consciousness changes it could not be transferred to anything else (another body such as a cat or another human being).

So Locke allows that in some extreme circumstances we might agree that a person is not the person that they were, but in general memory is sufficiently good enough to allow for continuity.

c) Enduring self

But for many Locke's notion of personhood fails to give sufficient account of the uniqueness of each individual. For example, if shortly after I rob a bank I suddenly lose my memory, could I claim that the person who committed the crime was not me but someone else? Or if I look at a picture which my parents tell me is of me aged four but have no recollection of that time, do I regard the child as a different person from me? The alternative to Locke's argument is to propose an enduring self or soul. The characteristic of the soul is that it is a **single substance** and unlike bodies which are composite it cannot change.

Key words

Mind–body **dualists** believe that souls and bodies are made of quite different substances.

Vitalism is the view that for the human body to be alive it must also possess a soul.

There are many theories about the nature of an enduring self. For **dualists** such as **Plato** (427–347BC) and **Descartes** (1597–1650) as the soul is quite distinct from the body a person remains a person whatever state their body is in. This view supports the **vitalist** position. But not everyone who believes in an enduring self is necessarily a dualist.

Aristotle (384–322BC) argued that the soul is the primary dynamic 'animating' principle of the body which enables it to fulfil its **potential**. In philosophical terms he said that the soul is the form of the body but without the body the soul is not able to exist. The process of being a person is a whole lifetime's activity; as he says, using a popular proverb, 'one swallow does not make a summer' (*Ethics* I: 1098a27).

d) Potential and actual persons

One of the problems faced by **Cartesian** dualists is an **epistemological** one. The question is how we can know whether a fully functioning body does or does not possess a soul. For example an android built to function fully as a human being and possessing all the necessary characteristics outlined above (see page 18) need not have a soul. I might argue that because it behaves just like me, and I know I have a soul, then it *must* have one also. But arguing from the particular to the general does not confirm the truth, it merely sets up a supposition which cannot be tested.

A problem faced by Aristotelians is **ensoulment**; that is, the moment when the human being receives its soul. **Aquinas** (*Summa Theologica* 1a Q76), for example, follows Aristotle's notion that the characteristic of soul is rationality but it only functions as such when attached to the body. For like Aristotle he agrees that as the soul is the first principle of the body, then a body without a rational soul is not fully a human person. Unlike Aristotle, though, he argued that the soul can exist separately from the body but as an incomplete person; only at the resurrection is the soul reunited with the body to become a person again.

Aquinas follows Aristotle's notion that the generative force is transmitted from the soul of the father through his sperm which then develops in the womb. As the foetus develops the soul animates it at the vegetative and animal levels until it is fully formed, at which stage it gains its intellectual or rational soul. For boys this is at 40 days and girls 90 days. Aquinas argues that the intellectual soul is given by God, whereas for Aristotle it is part of the natural process. Either way the foetus does not become an actual human person until some time after conception. This notion of **delayed ensoulment** is significant for many ethical debates today.

In the modern Roman Catholic tradition ensoulment occurs at the moment of conception. The embryo is not at this stage a 'person' in its fullest sense, because although it has the potential to be so, the process is a long one. In Aristotelian terms the actualisation process is a journey from embryo to foetus to baby to child to adulthood. Each stage seamlessly gives rise to the next. A few cells does not constitute an actual person, but has the potential to become so. In the official instruction *Donum Vitae* (1987) the

Key words

Cartesian is the adjective describing those who follow Descartes' philosophy.

Epistemology means the study of knowledge.

Cross-reference

For the moral significance of ensoulment see Chapter 3 on the problem of abortion and Chapters 5–6 for experiments on the early embryo.

Pope comments that observation of the physical state of the embryo is not sufficient to determine whether it is or is not a person:

> No experiment datum can be in itself sufficient to bring us to the recognition of a spiritual soul.
>
> (*Donum Vitae*, Chapter 1, paragraph 1)

e) Critique

- **Rationality and competency.** Locke's notion of personhood has been adopted by radical liberal Christian thinkers such as Joseph Fletcher as well as secular thinkers such as Peter Singer. But its problem is that it leads logically to contradictory ethical views about the treatment of people. For example if a person is defined as being a conscious rational being then infanticide (the killing of very young children) and non-voluntary euthanasia of senile and non-communicative humans is justified. But this is contrary to the Christian teaching on the protection of the weak and the ancient prohibition of infanticide. Furthermore, it defines rationality in a very narrow sense, when in Aquinas' terms having a 'rational nature' is not the same as being rational. In other words, competency and rationality are too particular and open to misuse when defining human persons and how to treat them.
- **Monozygotic twins.** The criticism of any form of vitalist position is posed by the problem that it is possible within the first 14 days of its development for an embryo to split and become another human being (as an identical or monozygotic twin). This suggests that the embryo up to this stage is either a human being (being genetically a member of *homo sapiens*) but not a human person, or neither a human being nor person. Once it is accepted that personhood and being a member of homo sapiens are not the same, then the moral status of human beings can be differentiated.

2 Sanctity of life arguments

Key question

How is the value of a person's life to be decided?

There is special status given to persons over and above the value of other animals and plant life. But how is the value of a person's life to be decided? The traditional position is referred to as the sanctity of life. Sanctity of life appears in various versions, both religious and non-religious or humanist. The religious version is that exemplified in the West by Christianity as a 'revealed law' and 'natural law' and the non-religious position by the philosopher Kant.

a) Kant's sanctity of life argument

Kant's argument for the sanctity of life may owe its outlook to his Christian upbringing but his argument is based neither on revealed

Key people

Immanuel Kant (1724–1804) sets out his moral philosophy in a number of books. The arguments here are taken from his *Grounding for the Metaphysics of Morals* (translated by James W. Ellington).

Cross-reference

For a more detailed explanation of Kant's ethic theory read Mel Thompson, *Ethical Theory*, Chapter 10.

nor natural law but on what he calls **moral law**. Moral law is derived by our powers of reason from the **good will**. The good will cannot be proved because it is just something we have and which defines us as human beings. This notion is the bedrock to Kant's subsequent ethical theory. As the good will is an intrinsic property of being human it follows that all our moral decisions must assume that whatever is good for me must consistently and **universally** be good for all. The categorical imperative is, therefore, the exercise of the good will universally. Kant stated the categorical imperative in many different ways but two are particularly important in expressing his idea of the sanctity of life:

1   The **practical imperative** expresses what Kant considered to be very important, and that is that people should never be treated as a means to an end but as an end in themselves or as Kant states it:

> *Act in such a way that you treat humanity, whether in your own person or in the person of another, always at the same time as an end never simply as a means.*
>
> (Immanuel Kant, *Grounding for the Metaphysics of Morals*, paragraph 429)

In other words when we will our neighbour's good we do so for no other reason than that they are a fellow human being. Obedience to the categorical imperative, Kant argues, is because it ensures that we treat all humans with equal **dignity**. No law or action may treat a person as less than a person or as an instrument to some other purpose. Kant entirely rejects the utilitarian view that in some cases a life may be worth less if it cannot yield more benefit than another.

2   The **kingdom of ends** expresses Kant's view that every rational being is capable of being a law maker whose **autonomous** decision takes into account the desire of being a member of the kingdom of ends. Kant defines the kingdom as 'a systematic union of different rational beings through common laws' (*Grounding*, paragraph 433). The kingdom of ends is an *idea* where all rational beings (humans) have equal dignity as law makers and law doers.

> *Act in accordance with the maxims of a member legislating universal laws for a merely possible kingdom of ends.*
>
> (Immanuel Kant, *Grounding for the Metaphysics of Morals*, paragraph 438)

The practical imperative and kingdom of ends therefore strongly support the notion that our lives are not ours to dispose of when we wish. This is why he rejects **suicide**. In Kant's example the

Key word

Maxim. Kant defines maxim as a 'subjective principle of acting' that is a general rule or principle governing the action of all rational people.

Cross-reference

For further discussion on suicide, read Michael Wilcockson, *Issues of Life and Death*, Chapter 2.

person feels that he has the right to shorten his life if continuing to live would only lead to more misery. But on reflection he realises that if this **maxim** were to become a universal law then he would be willing both a principle which would promote future life and also a law which would cut it short. This is a rational contradiction and he resolves it in favour of preserving life. And so Kant concludes, 'such a maxim cannot possibly hold as a universal law of nature and is, consequently, wholly opposed to the supreme principle of all duty' (*Grounding*, paragraph 422).

i) Critique of Kant

- **Reason or people.** Kant places such emphasis on reason and duty keeping that he appears to contradict the practical imperative. For example: do I always tell the truth even if this leads to innocent people being harmed or killed? If truth telling is to be preferred, then human life is not as intrinsically worthwhile as Kant suggests.
- **Clashing duties.** As Kant gives no clear way of deciding how to obey two equally demanding duties then we many prefer to adopt W.D. Ross' system of prima facie duties. Ross' system simply states that in some circumstances it will be clear that some duties are more appropriate than others. But as Kant views this as undermining the absoluteness of the categorical imperative it has to be assumed that for Kant a life may have to be sacrificed for principle and this appears to contradict the essence of his moral theory.

b) Natural law sanctity of life arguments

Cross-reference

For a more detailed account of natural law read Mel Thompson, *Ethical Theory*, Chapter 7.

Key quote

Cicero's widely accepted definition of natural law is:

True law is right reason in agreement with nature. It is applied universally and is unchanging and everlasting.

CICERO, *DE RE PUBLICA* (55–52BC)

Aristotle argued that all things are created with a distinctive purpose. The purpose or 'final cause' (the *telos*) marks a stage when a thing or person is most fully functioning as it is intended. For **Aquinas**, God is the efficient cause of nature, so the world is purposeful and designed. Everything has a *telos* which it aims to fulfil but the primary purposes of human life are:

- self preservation, progress and reproduction
- self perfection (the pursuit of justice)
- to learn and live by reason
- to live in an ordered society
- to worship God.

Aquinas goes further. He argues that, although there are **primary principles** which always remain the same, there are many **secondary principles** which although they are derived from first order laws may not always be as binding.

- He allows for **situation** to alter secondary precepts.
- He also allows that some things may be right **in proportion** to a given end.

Natural law, though, does not think that all human life should be preserved at all costs. For example if the aim is to establish peace and restore justice, then life may be taken if it discriminates in favour of those who are innocent and those who are not and is proportionate to these ends.

This establishes an important natural law principle that **innocent human life must be preserved**. However, there is much debate about what constitutes an innocent life. Augustine argued that self-defence was not sufficient reason to kill an aggressor, but **Francisco de Vitoria** (1486–1546) defined a non-innocent life in terms of someone who intentionally intends harm. The principle of proportionality crucially ensures that the **intention** of the person protecting an innocent life is that and no more (for example, revenge). Natural law ethicists argue, therefore, that the aggressor loses the right to the protection of his life.

More problematic is whether the killing of innocent life is ever justified. Aquinas developed what has been termed the **doctrine of double effect** which permits the killing of an innocent life if it is not the primary intention and it is not disproportionate to the good ends. For example, a woman whose life is threatened by an ectopic pregnancy may remove the foetus even though this will almost certainly kill the baby. Every attempt should be made to save the life of the baby but the primary intention to save the mother's life by giving her treatment is not disproportionate to the unwilled death of the foetus.

Cross-reference

Read pages 54–55 below about how the doctrine of double effect makes an important contribution to the euthanasia debate.

i) Critique of natural law

- **Naturalistic fallacy.** For many ethicists, natural law suffers from the category mistake of deriving an 'ought from an is' (sometimes referred to as the naturalistic fallacy). This is particularly the case now that most biologists do not think that every aspect of nature is designed to have a particular purpose.
- **Casuistry.** Casuistry means law making, but it is often used negatively to mean the use of clever arguments to get round a legal problem. The doctrine of double effect is in effect a utilitarian argument, even though it tries to maintain the sanctity of life principle.

c) Revealed ethics sanctity of life arguments

Within Christianity there are many versions of the sanctity of life argument because, although the basic proposition is that life is **sacred** and given to humans by God, modern medical advances have made it increasingly more difficult to determine whether a person has reached a stage where 'life', in any proper sense of the notion, is still a life. Those who hold to a **strong sanctity of life** view fiercely defend the sanctity of life against all humanistic or utilitarian effects which attempt to dilute or modify it. A number of terms are used to define their position. Sometimes, especially in political circles, this is called the **pro-life** position and in philosophical terms such a view corresponds to **vitalism**. Vitalists argue that a human life is always sacred because it possesses a soul and that there are no **ordinary or extraordinary** means which justify the termination of a human life – even from the moment of conception.

Sanctity of life is defined according to **revealed ethics** by the following biblical texts:

- **Set apart**: In Christian thought every human being is created in the image and likeness of God. To be created in God's image implies that humans are set apart and different from all other creatures and that every human being possesses a 'spark' of divinity (Genesis 1:27) within them which sets them apart from other creatures (Genesis 1:28). The **incarnation** of the Word of God as man in the person of Jesus (John 1:14) reaffirms the sanctity, **holiness** and **intrinsic value** of every human life **unconditionally** in its relationship with God.

- **Loan and destiny**: If God is the author of life then it follows that he is the one who determines when it should end (Job 1:21). It is not up to the individual whether he or she might add or subtract from his or her life or anyone else's because life is a gift, or a loan, from God. God is a providential God who through nature or other means is the only being who may directly terminate a person's life.

- **Respect and honour**: Taking a life is broader than simply killing and the prohibition in the Ten Commandments (Exodus 20:13) not to murder is part of the social glue which equally shows respect for parents, property, marriage, husband and neighbour. The command in Deuteronomy 30:19–20 to 'choose life' is the believer's response to honour God and respect life.

- **Love and protection**: Love requires the Christian to respect and protect all humans regardless of status, gender and age. This is famously illustrated in Jesus' parable of the Good Samaritan (Luke 10:29–37). The Greek term often used by the New Testament is **agape** and in its Christian usage suggests that love is active (1 Corinthians 13:6) and requires a person to sacrifice his own greatest happiness for others. Jesus' life is an explicit reminder that life is God's gift of love (John 3:16).

But for many Christians sanctity of life in addition to revealed law is also supported by natural law. This is the **Roman Catholic** view as set out by Pope John Paul II in *Evangelium Vitae* (1995). *Evangelium Vitae* considers how contemporary society has undermined the sanctity of life and by developing a 'culture of death' has devalued the dignity of human life. In particular it has marginalised the weak, the ill and the handicapped.

In the Protestant Christian tradition **Karl Barth** (1886–1968) used his version of **divine command theory** based both on the natural order and revealed law that suicide is self-murder and wrong, although in some extreme circumstances God could command someone to take a life.

The main problems of sanctity of life lie not so much in the principles but in the applications to situations which become more and more complicated as medical science blurs the boundaries between life and death. Some supporters of sanctity of life appeal to **extraordinary means** as a justification for killing when someone is no longer able to live a worthwhile life, due perhaps to extreme suffering or irreversible brain damage.

In these cases those who support a **weak sanctity of life** argue that agape should be the primary determining principle. The weak sanctity of life view argues that being alive, in a Christian sense, means being able to live life in body and soul as a 'living sacrifice' (Romans 12:1). Being 'alive' is not sufficient unless a person can express himself physically *and* spiritually.

Some warn against making life so absolute that it turns it into an idol worthy of worship. As **Stanley Hauerwas** has argued, as the Church has allowed martyrdom on occasions then the sanctity of life principle is not so absolute and permits taking life when it is for the well-being of others. He concludes:

Appeals to the sanctity of life as an ideology make it appear that Christians are committed to the proposition that there is nothing in life worth dying for.

(Stanley Hauerwas, *Suffering Presence*, page 92)

i) Critique of revealed ethics

- If shortening life is against sanctity of life, then as Hume argues is prolonging it also bad?
- If life is a gift then isn't it mine to do with as I wish?
- People don't actually believe in the sanctity of life because they frequently find reasons to make it less absolute. The weak sanctity of life is a good example of this, but as Peter Singer argues, the next logical step is that it should be replaced by a non-religious rational quality of life criterion.

3 Quality of life arguments

Quality of life arguments take an **instrumentalist** view of human life. In other words a life is only worthwhile if it can fulfil those things which make life worth living. There is nothing intrinsically good about being alive except as a means of enabling us to experience those things which are desired.

a) Peter Singer

Peter Singer is a prominent philosopher who has strongly argued that it is time now to abandon the sanctity of life principle in favour of the non-religious quality of life argument. Singer's arguments develop Locke's notion that the value of life depends on a person's ability to have desires and preferences and not on some mystical 'enduring self' which automatically gives priority to humans above all other animals. In *Rethinking Life and Death* (1995) Singer sets out his five new rational quality of life commandments to replace those of the traditional sanctity of life position:

- *Recognise that the worth of human life varies*
- *Take responsibility for the consequences of your decision*
- *Respect a person's desire to live or die*
- *Bring children into the world only if they are wanted*
- *Do not discriminate on the basis of species*
       (from Peter Singer, *Rethinking Life and Death*, pages 190–202)

In 1983 Singer caused controversy with the following comment on the Baby Doe abortion case in the USA:

If we compare a severely defective human infant with a nonhuman animal, a dog or a pig, for example, we will often find the non human to have superior capacities, both actual and potential, for rationality, self-consciousness, communication, and anything else that can plausibly be considered morally significant.
       (quoted also in Peter Singer, *Rethinking Life and Death*, page 201)

Peter Singer

Peter Singer was born in Melbourne, Australia, in 1946, and educated at the University of Melbourne and the University of Oxford. He was the director of the Centre for Human Bioethics, Monash University, and since 1999 he has been Ira W. DeCamp Professor of Bioethics in the University Center for Human Values at Princeton University. Outside academic work he is the co-founder, and President, of The Great Ape Project, an international effort to obtain basic rights for chimpanzees, gorillas and orangutans. He is also President of Animal Rights International.

The following is Peter Singer's own summary of his philosophical position, 'a philosophical self portrait':

'The ultimate practical question is: "How are we to live?" To give a general answer to such a broad question is, however, a daunting task, and most of my writing has focused on more specific practical questions.

I am probably best known for Animal Liberation, 1st edn 1975, 2nd edn 1990, a book that gave its title to a worldwide movement. The essential philosophical view it maintains is simple but revolutionary. Species is, in itself, as irrelevant to moral status as race or sex. Hence all beings with interests are entitled to equal consideration: that is, we should not give their interests any less consideration than we give to the similar interests of members of our own species. Taken seriously, this conclusion requires radical changes in almost every interaction we have with animals, including our diet, our economy, and our relations with the natural environment.

To say that this idea is revolutionary is not to say that it was especially novel. Similar ideas can be found, for instance, in Henry Salt's Animals' Rights, first published in 1892. My contribution was to restate this view clearly and rigorously, and to illustrate that alternative views are based on self-interest, either naked or disguised by religious or other myths.

My broader credo can be found in Practical Ethics, 1st edn 1979, 2nd edn 1993. Here the treatment of animals receives its proper place, as one among several major ethical issues. I approach each issue by seeking the solution that has the best consequences for all affected. By "best consequences", I understand that which satisfies the most preferences, weighted in accordance with the strength of the preferences. Thus my ethical position is a form of preference-utilitarianism.

In Practical Ethics I apply this ethic to such issues as equality (both between humans, and between humans and non-human animals), abortion, euthanasia and infanticide, the obligations of the wealthy to those who are living in poverty, the refugee question, our interactions with non-human beings and ecological systems, and obedience to the law. A non-speciesist and consequentialist approach to these issues leads to striking conclusions. It offers a clear-cut account of why abortion is ethically justifiable, and an equally clear condemnation of our failure to share our wealth with people who are in desperate need.

Some of my conclusions have been found shocking, and not only in respect of animals. In Germany, my advocacy of active euthanasia for severely disabled newborn infants has generated heated controversy. I first discussed this in Practical Ethics; later, as co-author, with Helga Kuhse, in Should the Baby Live?, 1985; and most recently in Rethinking Life and Death, 1995. Perhaps it is only to be expected, though, that there should be heated opposition to an ethic that challenges the hitherto generally accepted ethical superiority of human beings, and the traditional view of the sanctity of human life.'

(Peter Singer in Thomas Mautner, The Penguin Dictionary of Philosophy (1997), pages 521–522)

b) Utilitarian quality of life arguments

So what 'goods' make life worthwhile? **Utilitarianism** is a modern non-religious ethic which offers a clear maxim that what makes life worthwhile is when the greatest happiness is achieved for the greatest number of people. This appears to offer a rational means by which to judge the quality of an individual's life within the context of society and is frequently used in the context of medical ethics.

Cross-reference

For a more detailed account of utilitarianism read Mel Thompson, *Ethical Theory*, Chapter 9.

However, despite its seemingly simple aims, utilitarian philosophers offer several different versions of the maxim and therefore what is meant by quality of life.

Key people

Jeremy Bentham (1748–1832) was a British philosopher. He used utilitarianism as a rational means of reforming the law.

- **Hedonic utilitarians**, such as **Jeremy Bentham**, argue that the quality of life is judged when the amount of pleasure achieved is greater than any experience of pain. Judging a worthwhile life therefore is highly subjective both from the individual's point of view and from the perspective of others. Bentham suggested that pain and pleasure could in some sense be calculated in terms of duration, intensity and those affected. But even if this could be done, many utilitarians argue that there is more to life than pleasure and absence of pain.

- **Preference satisfaction utilitarians** such as Peter Singer argue that the quality of life is to be judged against whatever people consider to be the most desirable – and that might equally be wanting to live as to die. Preferences might also include other feelings such as generosity and altruism. For example being tortured in war for one's country would not usually be considered pleasurable but as a duty to others it is a preference which significantly makes a valuable contribution to society.

- **Ideal utilitarians** such as **G.E. Moore** argue that the problem with preference utilitarianism is that there is no means by which to judge the usefulness of one preference over another. There are some goods such as justice and beauty which are generally regarded to be of higher quality than the lower qualities such as pleasure.

Key people

G.E. Moore (1873–1958) was a British philosopher. In his most influential book *Principia Ethica* (1903) he argued that goodness is a special non-natural quality which can only be known through intuition and especially in the experience of beauty and friendship.

Robert Goodin is professor of both social and political theory and philosophy at the Research School of Social Sciences, Australian National University. His argument for welfare utilitarianism may be found in Peter Singer's *A Companion to Ethics* (Blackwell, 1993).

- **Welfare utilitarians** such as **Robert Goodin** argue that although the ideal utilitarians are right to say that there are some goods which are more valuable than others they have made these qualities too abstract. For utilitarianism to work we need to be able to deal with qualities that can be demonstrated to enhance human society. These, he suggests, are general welfare preferences such as health, money, shelter and food. An important feature of welfare utilitarianism is that it gives a concrete **duty** to all in society to provide for all its members. So, for example, a welfare utilitarian doctor might choose to overrule a patient's preference to refuse medication and die in favour of medicines which he knows will have long-term good effects.

i) Critique of utilitarianism

There are many criticisms of utilitarianism but those which are the most important in terms of the quality of life argument and medical ethics are:

- The principle of utility **dehumanises** others by making them a means to an end. Kant influentially dismissed utilitarianism on the grounds that it failed to treat people as an end in themselves.

- The maxim is too subjective and gives no clear account of what is meant by a valuable life. Pleasure is too limited a view of human desires and determining what someone does or does not prefer is often very difficult. In many cases people don't know what they prefer.

- A development of Kant's view by **Bernard Williams** is that utilitarianism can erode personal **integrity**. In Williams' imaginary example of Jim and the Indians (*Utilitarianism*, pages 98–99), Jim is given the choice either to kill one Indian himself and save twenty or refuse and see them all killed. Williams argues that, although the utilitarian answer is that Jim should kill one Indian himself, utilitarians fail to account for the effects of his action on his character. These moral feelings form just as much a part of the calculation of his action as the ends but utilitarians are not able to give a rational reason to include them.

Key people

Sir Bernard Williams
(1929–2003) was one of Britain's most influential philosophers and wrote on the philosophy of personal identity and ethics. In *Utilitarianism For and Against* (1973) he argues against J.C.C. Smart that utilitarianism offers the best form of ethics.

Summary diagram

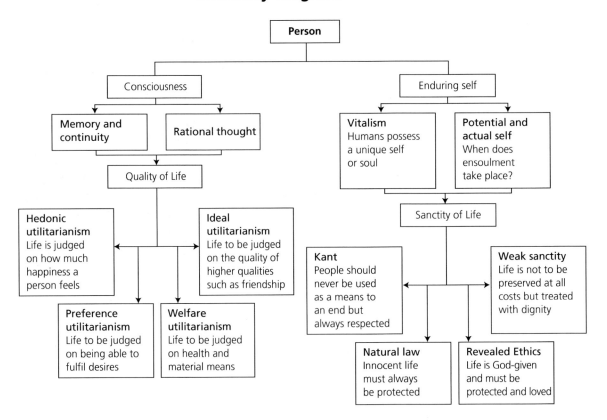

Study guide

By the end of this chapter you should have considered various reasons why people have adopted a sanctity of life argument, either based on revealed ethics, universal duty (Kant) or on the natural law view of protection of the innocent. You should also have considered why some have rejected the sanctity of life arguments in favour of quality of life arguments. Both arguments depend on what it means to exist as a person, whether humans have a soul or enduring self which makes them intrinsically worthwhile or whether we are a simple bundle of qualities none of which make us uniquely humans.

Revision checklist

Can you explain the meaning of:

■ necessary and sufficient conditions
■ the string quartet analogy and the problem with Locke's idea of identity
■ Aristotle's notion of the soul
■ the weak sanctity of life argument.

Can you explain:

■ Locke's definition of person
■ how Aquinas' natural law principle argues for the absolute protection of innocent life
■ the difference between actual and potential person arguments
■ the extrinsic factors Peter Singer uses to produce a coherent quality of life argument.

Can you explain why:

■ bodily change and continuity is a problem for Locke's theory
■ Aristotle's notion of the soul is an animating first principle of the body
■ Aquinas' idea of soul is slightly different from Aristotle's idea of soul.

Can you give arguments for and against:

■ using the double effect to justify unintended negative side effects
■ Kant's sanctity of life argument and the universal good will
■ having a strong sanctity of life argument
■ having a quality of life argument.

Essay question

1a. Explain what is meant by the sanctity of life.

1b. Assess the view that if shortening a life is against the sanctity of life principle then it is also wrong to prolong it.

The first part of the essay could outline the revealed or religious views as set out in the Bible, ensuring that it distinguishes between the strong and weak views. Make sure that you quote and explain key texts from the Bible. Explaining appropriate texts demonstrates knowledge and understanding. The revealed view could lead on to discuss Kant and his rational view that all human life must be treated as an end in itself. Finally, the natural law position can be considered by referring to Aquinas and his five primary precepts.

It might be helpful to begin with Hume's criticism (on which this question is based) that if the strong sanctity of life forbids interfering either with nature or God's wishes then it follows that the deliberate shortening of life is as bad as lengthening it. The evaluative element is the issue of whether shortening a life is morally equivalent to lengthening. The argument might then consider what it means to live a worthwhile life. The discussion might focus on whether it is possible to make judgements about the quality of a person's life and if so whether prolonging a life might indeed be as bad as shortening if this increases pain, for example.

Further essay questions

2a   Explain the difference between an actual and potential person.

2b   'At the moment of conception the human embryo is a person.' Discuss.

3   To what extent does Locke's definition of personhood offer the most coherent basis for medical ethics today?

4   'Without the principle of the sanctity of life there would be no respect for persons.' Discuss.

3 ABORTION

Chapter checklist ✓

This chapter considers whether having a child is a right or a gift. However, if it is a mother's right to have a child is it equally her right to terminate a pregnancy if she wishes? Abortion is discussed with reference to a woman's right to privacy, autonomy, the abortion pill and the problem of when a foetus becomes a person with rights. Several normative ethic systems and their views on abortion are considered.

1 Women's autonomy and rights

Case study
Two cases of abortion

In 1962 a patient in a state mental hospital raped a fellow patient, an unmarried girl ill with a radical schizophrenic psychosis. The victim's father, learning what had happened, charged the hospital with culpable negligence and requested that an abortion to end an unwanted pregnancy be performed at once, in an early stage of the embryo. The staff and administrators of the hospital refused to do so, on the ground that the criminal law forbids all abortion except 'therapeutic' ones when the mother's life is at stake – because the moral law, it is supposed, holds that any interference with an embryo after fertilisation is murder, i.e. the taking of an innocent human being's life...

Even self-defence legalism would have allowed the girl to kill her attacker, no matter that he was innocent in the forum of conscience because of his madness. The embryo is no more innocent, no less an aggressor or unwelcome invader! Is not the most loving thing possible (the right thing) in this case a responsible decision to terminate the pregnancy?

(Joseph Fletcher, *Situationism*, pages 37–39)

> *The abortion debate intensified yesterday when the Rev. Joanna Jepson failed in her attempt to bring criminal charges against two doctors involved in a 'late' abortion on an unborn child with a cleft lip and palate.*
>
> *The Crown Prosecution Service said it was satisfied that the doctors involved in the abortion on a woman more than 24 weeks pregnant had acted in good faith and there would be no prosecution. The CPS inquiry into the case in Herefordshire reopened after a judicial review sought by Miss Jepson, 28, who had a successful operation on a jaw deformity and whose brother has Down's syndrome.*
>
> ('Vicar loses court battle to prosecute doctors over abortions', *Daily Telegraph*, 17 March 2005)

In both of these cases the solution to a social problem was solved using abortion. But are the moral reasons equally weighted and equally persuasive? What, if anything, does it say about a society that allows abortion for a cleft lip and another society which refuses abortion even though a schizophrenic girl was raped?

In 2004 the abortion rate rose 2.1 per cent to 17.8 per 1000 women aged 15 to 44, the highest recorded in England and Wales. In other words 185,415 women resident in England and Wales had an abortion in 2004, compared to 181,600 in 2003. Ann Furedi's response recorded in *The Times* is typical of those who see the issue primarily in terms of a woman's right to choose whether she wishes to have a baby or not.

Key quote

We should stop seeing abortion as a problem and start seeing it as a legitimate and sensible solution to the problem of unwanted pregnancy.

ANN FUREDI, BRITISH PREGNANCY ADVISORY SERVICE

> *'Women today want to plan their families and, when contraception fails, they are prepared to use abortion to get back in control of their lives,' Ms Furedi (British Pregnancy Advisory Service) said. 'Motherhood is just one among many options open to women and it is not surprising that younger women want to prioritise other things. We should stop seeing abortion as a problem and start seeing it as a legitimate and sensible solution to the problem of unwanted pregnancy.'*
>
> ('Abortions soar as careers come first', *The Times*, 28 July 2005)

Key question

Consider the feminist philosopher Ellen Willis' question:

Can it be moral, under any circumstances, to make a woman bear a child against her will?

VILLAGE VOICE (16 JULY, 1985, PAGE 15)

For many women abortion is more than just a debate about the status of the foetus, and rather about the place of women in society and their ability to determine the kinds of lives they wish to live. Ellen Willis' answer to her question (see margin) is that until women have the same autonomy as men the answer is that it is always wrong to make a woman have a baby against her will. Nevertheless, not all feminists think the same and many have to grapple with the view that the unborn child may also have rights as well. The question, therefore, is how to balance these against the rights of women.

a) Foetus' right to life vs woman's right to bodily integrity

One of the most influential arguments is by the philosopher **Judith Jarvis Thomson** in *A Defence of Abortion* (1971). Her argument focuses primarily on rape cases or faulty contraception where a woman finds herself pregnant against her will. In it she argues that:

- A woman **owns** her body, in the same way that we might say she owns her own house or owns her own life. Therefore as a woman she has a *prior* claim to her body before pregnancy so she may remove the foetus any time she wants.
- An unwanted pregnancy poses an enormous strain on a woman's body. She is entitled to some form of **self-defence** even if this means the 'direct killing' of an innocent party.
- Foetal rights and the mother's rights **are not equal**. The foetus does have rights but they cannot be equivalent to the mother, even though the foetus is innocent. The mother and foetus are not two tenants in the same house rented by both. The foetus is using the mother's body and therefore has tenant's rights not ownership rights. She may choose to acknowledge the rights of the foetus but she is not compelled to do so. Having a right to life does not give one a right to use someone else's body.
- There is no law or prima facie duty which **compels the woman to be a good Samaritan** especially at her own expense. It may of course be prima facie wrong for a woman to abort having had voluntary intercourse, but not necessarily a breach of her rights.

b) A woman's prima facie right to privacy

Cross-reference

Read page 6 on prima facie rights and duties.

The problem with Thomson's argument is that although it may justify foetal *extractions* it does not necessarily justify foetal *extinctions*. Other feminists argue therefore that the issue is not so much about body integrity but a woman's prima facie right to privacy to decide on their own and their unborn foetus' best interests; that will usually mean the death of the foetus.

Christine Overall (*Human Reproduction: Principles, Practices and Policies*, 1993) argues that it is morally wrong not to respect the private wishes of the mother even if she wishes to kill the foetus. Her argument is:

- keeping the foetus alive against the mother's wish violates the **reproductive autonomy** of the mother; she has a right to break her genetic obligations to the foetus as well as her social duties
- the mother's genetic relationship to the foetus makes her the most appropriate person to decide on its best interests – and that will usually result in death

- making her keep the foetus would be like compelling her to give up one of her organs against her will; there is nothing to justify an intrusion into her privacy of this kind
- removing her right to decide on the fate of the foetus is another example of a patriarchal society which treats women as being incapable of deciding on their own reproductive status.

c) Early abortions and RU-486

Many of the arguments above apply to later abortions where the status of the foetus is more contentious. So the prospect of using the 'abortion pill' **RU-486** for early abortions is attractive.

Its chief advantages are that it is:

- less traumatic than surgery
- available to more women; women don't have to travel so far to a clinic
- less expensive than other forms of abortion
- intended to leave women more in control of the process
- private and out of the gaze of anti-abortionists.

But it has not met with complete favour. Some argue that in fact by making abortion too easily available it actually reduces women's autonomy. Many women feel that the pressure from pro-choice groups is to have an abortion rather than to be a mother. Real choice would mean providing the support of having a child without feeling that this has betrayed other women who want an abortion.

Finally some consider that the relative privacy of RU-486 hides the problem of unwanted pregnancy from men. As the process is hidden from them it trivialises the significance and possible trauma which an abortion entails leaving a woman more isolated and less able to ask for help.

2 The personhood problem

Key question

To what extent do you agree with this headline: 'This foetus is 20 weeks old and can be legally aborted...some scientists say she should have a painkiller first'

DAILY TELEGRAPH, OCTOBER 2000

Key word

Begging the question is when the conclusion is contained in one of the premises of the question.

For many people the abortion issue hinges on one important issue and that is establishing whether or not the foetus is a person. Once it can be established that the foetus is a person then it becomes entitled to the same **basic rights** of protection as any other person. If the foetus is not a person the abortion issue focuses on other contingent factors such as the psychological effects on the mother (and others) rather than on the foetus itself.

As we have seen in Chapter 2 the personhood problem also **begs the question**: what is a person? For those who argue for an **enduring self** the question is *when* does the foetus acquire a soul and, for those such as Locke and others who consider that the term 'person' refers to a **bundle** of characteristics, the question is when has the foetus acquired sufficient of these characteristics to be treated as a person.

a) Ensoulment at conception

Ensoulment at conception is supported by those who take a vitalist view of life. The attractiveness of this position is that as soon as conception takes place, what is created genetically could only be a member of *homo sapiens* and nothing else. For those, such as the Roman Catholic Church, who hold a natural law moral position, the life now formed is **innocent** and must be protected absolutely from the moment of conception. Conservative Christians also argue for ensoulment at conception based on biblical texts such as Psalm 139:13–16 and Jeremiah 20:16–18 where the writers speak of the special status of the foetus in the womb as created by God.

b) Delayed ensoulment

Delayed ensoulment (or progressive ensoulment) is supported by those who may still hold a vitalist position but who do not consider conception to be the moment of ensoulment. Aquinas' argument developed Aristotle's view that the foetus only acquires an intellectual soul once the vegetative and animal aspects of soul are fully developed, that is, at 40 days for boys and 90 days for girls. Although Aristotle and Aquinas were guessing as to when biologically the foetus acquired a soul, the notion of a delayed ensoulment is attractive to those who consider that there has to be more to a person than a few cells to support the functioning of the self (or soul). But the problem with this view (as much as it is for those who hold the 'bundle' view of self) in modern terms is to determine when, in biological terms, a 'soul' could emerge or be supported.

c) Primitive streak

Up to 14 days it is possible for **monozygotic twins** to develop and the **primitive streak** is now discernible. After this stage the foetus or foetuses develop **individually**. Some have referred to the foetus before this stage as the **pre-embryo** and in law experimentations are permitted to take place up to the fourteenth day.

d) Brain activity

Brain activity is important both for those who support delayed ensoulment and those such as Locke who consider consciousness as the essential characteristic of persons. The attractiveness of selecting brain activity as the start of life is that it not only uses the **cognitive criterion** as the start of life but that it can also be used as the criterion to determine the end of life. The problem here is whether

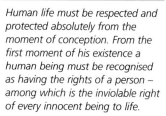

brain activity has to be continuous or whether life begins at the first spasmodic moment. Spasmodic brain activity occurs at 54 days, continuous brain function at 32 weeks. Less certain is whether brain activity is in any sense conscious and whether or not the foetus can feel pain. Some argue for a minimal case that it marks the first phase in consciousness, in the same way that a person could later fall into a coma and then recover.

e) Viability

Viability refers to the ability of the foetus or baby to become self-sufficient outside the womb. The older term 'quickening' was used to refer to the movement of the baby in the womb as a person but today the issue of viability has become a crucial one to determine the upper limit of abortion in legislation. At present UK law sets the upper limit for abortion at 24 weeks. The problem is that if modern neo-natal medicine is good enough to treat a baby of twenty weeks and enable it to survive then how is its status any different from a baby whose life is to be terminated? But viability is an elastic term: it could refer to any stage after birth, when the baby is not directly dependent on its mother, or to a stage when it could make decisions for itself. Some have argued that viability should be expressed in terms of being in the position of being able to have a reasonable **quality of life.** So a baby which is severely handicapped or severely diseased might be considered not to have a viable life, in which case abortion would be a reasonable decision.

3 The law and abortion

Key question

Should all abortions be available on demand? Is there a need to regulate abortion by law?

According to J.S. Mill's liberal principle, the law and the state should not interfere with private morality. As we have seen, many argue that abortion is essentially a private affair but, contrary to what many people may think, abortion is not available on demand in the UK. The law as it has evolved implicitly recognises the need to protect the life of the foetus but equally tries to balance this against harm done to the mother and existing children.

The **1967 Abortion Act** remains the foundation of the law but an important modification in 1990 resulted in two changes. Firstly, the upper limit was reduced from 28 to 24 weeks (on the basis that many foetuses were being aborted alive at 28 weeks) for most therapeutic abortions and, secondly, the implied sanctity of the baby's life was undermined by the change which permitted abortion of any handicapped child up to the moment of birth.

a) Legal grounds for abortion

Grounds for Abortion 1967 Abortion Act and amended under section 37 of the Human Fertilisation and Embryology Act 1990

A The continuance of the pregnancy would involve risk to the life of the pregnant woman greater than if the pregnancy were terminated;

B The termination is necessary to prevent grave permanent injury to the physical or mental health of the pregnant woman;

*C   The continuation of the pregnancy would involve risk greater than if the pregnancy were terminated, of injury to the physical or mental health of the pregnant woman;

*D   The continuance of the pregnancy would involve risk, greater than if the pregnancy were terminated, of injury to the physical or mental health of any existing child(ren) of the family of the pregnant woman;

E There is substantial risk that if the child were born it would suffer from such physical or mental abnormalities as to be seriously handicapped; *or in an emergency*:

F To save the life of the pregnant woman; or

G To prevent grave permanent injury to the physical or mental health of the pregnant woman.

- *Grounds C and D may take place up to 24 weeks. All other grounds are without time limit.
- Two doctors must give their assent to permit a doctor to carry out the abortion.
- A conscience clause permits a doctor to refuse to be involved with an abortion.

b) Abortion statistics

Abortion statistics, England and Wales: 2006

- The total number of abortions was 193,700, compared with 186,400 in 2005, a rise of 3.9%.
- The age-standardised abortion rate was 18.3 per 1,000 resident women aged 15–44, compared with 17.8 in 2005.
- The abortion rate was highest at 35 per 1,000, for women aged 19.
- The under-16 abortion rate was 3.9 and the under-18 rate was 18.2 per 1,000 women, both higher than in 2005.
- 87% of abortions were funded by the NHS; of these, just over half (55%) took place in the independent sector under NHS contract.
- 89% of abortions were carried out at under 13 weeks gestation; 68% were at under 10 weeks.
- Medical abortions accounted for 30% of the total compared with 24% in 2005.
- 2,000 abortions (1%) were on Grounds E, i.e. risk that the child would be born handicapped.

Source: Department of Health (issued 19 June 2007) Bulletin 2007/01
http://www.dh.gov.uk/en/Publicationsandstatistics/Publications/PublicationsStatistics/DH_075697

4 Normative ethical responses to abortion

Abortion touches on many of the key medical ethical issues looked at in Chapter 1. Beauchamp and Childress for example suggested **four principles**: respect for **autonomy** (freedom to exercise one's will), **non-maleficence** (avoiding harm), **beneficence** (producing benefits) and **justice** (distributing benefits, risks and costs fairly). Each of the normative ethical systems should be judged against these principles.

a) Natural law

Natural law arguments, as we have seen, argue that as a primary precept an innocent life should always be protected. Once the foetus is considered a person whether at conception or at brain activity for example (for those who prefer delayed ensoulment) its life becomes sacrosanct.

The Roman Catholic Church rules out delayed ensoulment for the following natural law reasons:

- God is the first cause of all human life as it is he who gives it life.
- Life therefore is a gift.
- Life at every stage offers the potential to become more fully actualised as a human being capable of loving and worshipping God.
- God therefore is also the final cause or *telos* of all human life.
- Although the embryo is not a fully flourishing person (any more than a one-year-old is) it has the potential to become so.
- Human life is to be seen as a **pilgrimage** in which the image of God emerges from the simplest physical form to the complex form *we* call 'person'.
- Humans therefore have an absolute responsibility to protect human life so that it may develop and flourish to its end or *telos*.

Does natural law permit any exceptions? Some suggest that, as natural law permits the killing of combatants in war, then by analogy an unwanted foetus might be considered an aggressor or trespasser in the womb of the mother. If so, then the foetus is no longer an innocent and subject to protection. But the analogy would only work in extreme cases (such as rape) and even then it hardly seems reasonable for the foetus to *intend* to harm the mother.

On the other hand the **doctrine of double effect** allows for some flexibility. For example, if a woman's life is threatened by an **ectopic pregnancy** or where a mother has uterine cancer, both may be treated if the primary intention is to treat the mother's health even if the unintended but foreseen *side-effect* kills the baby.

Key word

In **natural law** everything has its purpose or *telos*. Aquinas suggested that humans have five related primary ends. The spiritual *telos* is the worship of God. See page 23 above.

Key quote

If embryos are living, whether viable or not, they must be respected just like any other human person.

DONUM VITAE, 1987,
CHAPTER 1, PARAGRAPH 4

Key word

An **ectopic pregnancy** is where the foetus is developing in the fallopian tubes, not in the uterus. This usually proves fatal to mother and baby.

Technically, though, this is not an abortion (it is not deliberate killing) but a **termination**. In Roman Catholic teaching every effort should be made to preserve the life of the child.

b) Utilitarianism

Cross-reference

Read page 29 on the variety of utilitarianisms.

Utilitarian arguments all balance the good of keeping a child and the good of having an abortion. As we have seen, utilitarians vary as to what they think the 'good' is which should be maximised.

- **Hedonic utilitarians** argue that each case should be judged according to the amount of pain or happiness caused. There are many considerations here such as the emotional pain of bringing up an unwanted child, the financial costs of feeding and caring for another child which might affect the happiness of existing children and the restrictions placed on a woman who may wish to pursue a career. These all have to be balanced against the psychological harm caused by the loss of child (guilt, regret and reactions of others), the physical dangers caused by the abortion itself and the possible inability to have children in the future. Some might also consider the possible pain the foetus might go through – especially in the later stages of foetal development. This has become an increasingly significant part of the debate. Many scientists suggest that **sentience** in the sense of feeling pain occurs around twenty weeks, in which case at the very least the baby should be given an anaesthetic before being aborted.
- **Preference satisfaction utilitarians** argue that it is not just a question of balance of pain/happiness but what is desirable. Preference utilitarians take the preferences of the foetus more seriously than hedonic utilitarians, but only where they consider it would be reasonable for a foetus to have preferences. It would make sense, therefore, in cases of severe disability not to give a high value of life to the foetus as its desires would be far less than in a healthy foetus. It might even be considered that society would be better off without unwanted children or children who are a great drain on the financial and emotional well-being of society.
- **Ideal utilitarians** might well reject the quality of life arguments of the preference utilitarians and opt instead to balance ideals such as justice. They might for example consider that abortion merely as a form of contraception as a result of carelessness is hardly just grounds for terminating a life – especially in the later stages of pregnancy. On the other hand abortion on the grounds of rape or threats to a mother's life are justified measures against unwanted pregnancy. In either of the cases the question of justice cannot remain a purely private decision but must be consistent with the application of justice in other aspects of society.

- **Welfare utilitarians** argue that abortion has to be placed within the context of other medical needs. Although they might agree with the hedonic utilitarian that mental and physical concerns all have to be weighed up, it might also be considered that there should be careful counselling by a doctor and perhaps even a period of time to consider a decision before abortion itself. It might even be necessary for a doctor to over-rule a patient's preference in the best interests of the patient.

A general criticism of all utilitarian arguments is the vagueness of the 'threat' or 'pain' posed by a possible pregnancy as sufficient grounds for abortion. This is the problem of the **slippery slope**. Opponents argue that good reasons for abortion can quickly deteriorate to the trivial. For example the 1967 Abortion Act permits abortion on certain grounds as exceptions but, in practice, the statistics suggest that any woman who asks for an abortion is given it.

c) Virtue ethics

One reason why abortion causes considerable political disagreement is that it asks us to consider what kind of society we wish to be. Virtue ethics is not just about an individual's character but also the character of society. Do we want a society which uses killing (if that is how it is regarded) to solve social problems? And finally as abortion is also a medical procedure, it must also include the character and motives of the doctor.

- **Mother**. Virtue ethicists might argue that having an 'unwanted' child by avoiding abortion is not only a courageous act but also generous if followed by adoption. As we have seen many feminists argue that although there is no necessity to become a mother there is less justification to kill or terminate a life.
- **Society**. Some have argued that allowing abortion cultivates a 'culture of death'. Virtue ethics addresses the cold application of principles, whether they are consequential or deontological, from the point of view of the characteristics or traits we admire. As the philosopher Frankena has said, 'Principles without traits are impotent but traits without principles are blind'. As we have seen feminists are divided whether abortion enables women to choose their own destiny respectfully in society or whether, in fact, it places undue pressure on them to have abortions when they would rather continue with the pregnancy.
- **Doctor**. As Beauchamp and Childress have argued (see page 6 above) the four principles of doctors' ethics require also the right intentions such as kindness, courageousness, loving-kindness and open-mindedness. This might be hard for a doctor who

Key quote

Principles without traits are impotent but traits without principles are blind.

WILLIAM FRANKENA, *ETHICS*, PAGE 65

personally objects to abortion treating a woman who wants an abortion. It might equally be difficult for a doctor who considers abortion to be a symbol of autonomy or assumes that all rape victims should necessarily undergo abortion.

But as always with virtue ethical approaches the question is, how are the virtues to be decided? Some feel that there are particular female virtues which are undervalued by society and that until these are better represented abortion ethics, whether pro-life or pro-choice, will fail to deal with women's actual needs.

d) Revealed ethics

Cross-reference

The main elements of the strong sanctity of life argument are set out on pages 25–26 above.

- **Strong sanctity of life Christians** base their ethics primarily on the authority of the **Bible** and conclude that the Bible extends the command to 'love one's neighbour' to the child in the womb from the moment of conception. As all humans are made in the image of God (Genesis 1:27), the deliberate termination of an innocent life is a capital offence (Genesis 9:6) because only God can give and take away life (Job 1:21). Christ's life and death was so that Christians 'might have life and have it abundantly' (John 10:10). A key passage for Conservative Christians is **Exodus 21:21–25** which distinguishes between hitting a woman which causes her to miscarry the baby alive (punished with a fine) and verse 23 which states 'if any harm follows, then you shall give life for life'. Abortion, therefore, is murder and should be punished accordingly.

Cross-reference

The main elements of the weak sanctity of life argument are outlined on page 26 above.

- **Weak sanctity of life Christians** argue that abortion should be permitted only in rare cases where there is threat to the mother's mental or physical health. This view cuts across many Christian traditions and is the official view of the Church of England and the Methodist Church. Weak sanctity of life arguments might also support a delayed ensoulment view for early terminations but also warn that it is dangerous to make the life of the foetus so absolute that it becomes an idol. It therefore holds a **prima facie** view that the potential life of the foetus should be protected unless, as in the case of rape, it is more rational to prioritise the needs of the mother and existing family over the baby.

Key people

Joseph Fletcher's influential book on situationism, *Situation Ethics*, was published in 1966. In it he developed what he called his 'four working principles' which should be applied to each situation. These are: pragmatism (what is the most useful thing to do); relativism (there are no absolute laws); positivism (human laws must be based on reason – they are not God-given or natural); and personalism (all humans are to be treated as persons).

- **Liberal Christians** argue along consequential lines that the primary consideration is love or **agape. Joseph Fletcher** (1905–1991) called this view **situationism**. Fletcher outlines a case in 1962 where an unmarried, schizophrenic girl was raped by an inmate of the mental hospital where they both lived. However, her father's request for an abortion was denied because the only moral and legal grounds for abortion would have been if her life was in grave risk. Fletcher rejects the rigid deontological legalism or 'formalism' of Christians who place rules before

Key word

Antinomianism means no laws or rules.

people, but nor does he advocate **antinomianism**; instead he suggests that there should be **four working principles** which direct agape to its best end. In the case of the raped girl Fletcher argues that her mental health is paramount and, furthermore, 'no *unwanted and unintended* baby should ever be born'.

Summary diagram

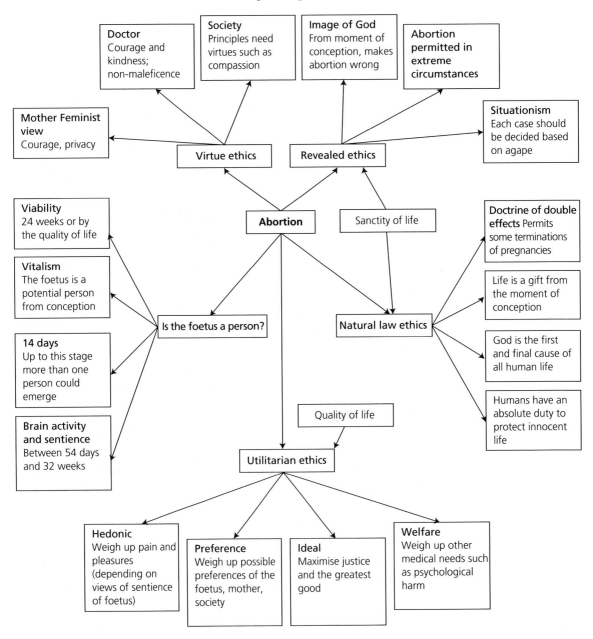

Study guide

By the end of this chapter you should have considered abortion from a variety of different moral view points. These should include the rights of the mother as well as the rights of the foetus. In addition you should have formed a view as to the status of the foetus as an actual or potential person. This should also mean reading the previous chapter and considering such issues as ensoulment and viability.

Revision checklist

Can you explain:

- natural law response to abortion
- the use of the double effect to justify terminations but *not* abortions
- the religious response to abortion, in particular strong and weak sanctity of life arguments
- Fletcher's four working principles in relation to abortion
- preference utilitarian consideration of the foetus' preferences vs preferences of the mother.

Do you know:

- what it means to say a woman has a prima facie right to privacy
- what RU-486 is and the moral and medical issues associated with it
- the law on abortion and the harm criterion (physical and mental)
- what welfare utilitarianism is and how it can be used to assess abortion.

Can you give arguments for and against the claim that:

- a foetus is a person at conception
- utilitarian arguments are effective in assessing abortion
- virtue ethics is an effective ethical system in assessing abortion
- a woman's right over her body justifies abortion
- virtue ethics is effective in deciding whether to have an abortion or not.

Essay question

1. 'The only situation which would justify abortion would be to save the mother's life.' Discuss.

The question suggests that you should be looking at this issue from several different ethical view points. Probably the best place to begin is with a normative system that considers abortion to be intrinsically wrong but is prepared to make exceptions in extreme circumstances. A sanctity of life argument usually considers the foetus' life to be intrinsically worthwhile and the Bible calls on it to be protected at all times. However, many would consider that a mother's life as an adult and in terms of developed consciousness to be more worthwhile. In extreme cases her life is to be preferred over her baby's life. This view might be contrasted with a natural law position which appears to regard the status of the foetus and the mother to be the same.

The judgement of the sanctity of life has to consider whether it is coherent to value the mother's life more than the foetus. This might be judged in terms of foetal development and the status of the foetus' consciousness. The argument might consider the consequentialist position to be clearer, that is, that to save the life of the mother makes more utilitarian sense than the loss of both. The natural law position might be considered using the doctrine of the double effect and the strengths and weaknesses of that view.

Further essay questions

2a   Explain the main aims of utilitarianism.
2b   Assess the view that utilitarianism is the best approach to abortion.

3a   Explain the arguments for when a human foetus could be considered a person.
3b   'Even potential human life must have absolute protection from harm.' Discuss.

4   Discuss the view that having an abortion is entirely a woman's choice.

Chapter checklist

The problem of euthanasia is reviewed, and the place of palliative care considered, beginning with the moral problems raised by suicide. The main distinction between cutting short a life and allowing to die is discussed with reference to consequential and deontological ethics. The chapter concludes by looking at the issue of non-voluntary euthanasia and the usefulness of virtue ethics for doctors in the application of prima facie duty to care for their patients.

Case study
Devoted husband kills wife

In May 2007 a newspaper headline read 'Devoted husband in "mercy killing" of depressed wife is found guilty of murder' (*The Daily Telegraph*). Frank Lund had been happily married to his wife for 33 years but she was severely depressed caused by an acute form of irritable bowel syndrome and had taken a large dose of pills. He bought the tablets for her but soon after taking them she began to be sick. He was afraid she would not die and because he had promised her that she would not wake up in hospital he put a plastic bag over her head and smothered her with a pillow.

The case is significant because groups campaigning for euthanasia did not give their support to Lund. Why was this? The answer is that Patricia Lund's condition was not life threatening and therefore Frank Lund's action was the direct and immediate cause of her death.

1 A problem of definition

Euthanasia means literally 'a good death' but should a person be allowed to choose when they die?

The case therefore raises a basic problem of distinguishing between the right to suicide, assisted suicide, euthanasia, murder and manslaughter (or involuntary homicide). This is not just confusing for those involved in making medical ethics decisions but also for what it implies about the way we view the value of life and the role of society.

- **Suicide** is when a person dies as a direct result of their own voluntary action.
- **Assisted suicide** is when a person dies as a direct result of their own voluntary action but with the help of another person. This is different from voluntary euthanasia only in so far as the person may have many reasons for wanting to die; their condition doesn't have to be life-threatening.
- **Physician-aided suicide** is when a person dies as a direct result of their own voluntary action but with the help of a doctor or physician.
- **Physician aid in dying** is when a person's death is hastened but not directly caused by the aid (e.g. medication) of a doctor or physician.
- **Voluntary euthanasia** is when a person's death is directly caused by another person (perhaps a doctor) on their request. Most arguments today assume that the person requesting to die is suffering from an underlying life-threatening condition and is in great pain.
- **Passive euthanasia** is when a doctor or physician withdraws life-sustaining treatment which indirectly causes death. Alternatively the physician allows a patient to die by 'letting nature take its course'.
- **Non-voluntary euthanasia** is when a doctor or the courts decide that life-sustaining treatment is no longer justified.

Palliative means giving pain-relieving care.

Many of these terms appear to be interchangeable. For example is passive euthanasia the same as physician aid in dying? Many people who support the view that a doctor may give **palliative** care which indirectly hastens death nevertheless resist calling this euthanasia. In their own mind this distinguishes between treatment, which is **passive** (indirect killing), and care, which is **active** (directly reducing pain).

Although the distinction between suicide and euthanasia is the involvement of another person, the fundamental issue is whether it is morally licit or permissible for a person to take their own life.

2 Ethics of suicide

Cross-reference

For a more detailed discussion of suicide read Michael Wilcockson, *Issues of Life and Death*, Chapter 2.

Key word

Abrogation means to defy a rule, duty or law and therefore to abolish.

It is important to distinguish between two kinds of suicide: **egoistical suicide** and **altruistic suicide**. This distinction is important in the present complex debate about euthanasia. Egoistical suicide leaves the choice entirely to the individual and in many philosophical and religious traditions this is considered to be selfish and wrong. The aim of altruistic suicide, on the other hand, is only indirectly to take one's own life and primarily for some greater cause which necessitates death as a side effect. The question of **volition** or what is willed or intended is an important ethical principle (especially for natural law and virtue ethics). Altruistic suicide is often more acceptable than egoistical suicide, but the distinction is less clear when applied to voluntary euthanasia.

Moral arguments against suicide are:

- **Suicide as an abrogation of duty to God.** In the Christian sanctity of life tradition, Augustine taught that suicide is blasphemy. Life is a gift from God and not ours to dispose of as we wish; therefore to will our own death defies God as the giver of life. Furthermore, as the person is unable to repent, they die in a state of mortal sin without the possibility of redemption.
- **Suicide as defiance against moral law.** Kant argued that suicide is not the result of a rationally free act. Although it might be understandable to say that out of self love I choose to end my life, my decision is being dictated by external factors (such as pain, unhappiness, lack of hope), not reason. According to the categorical imperative it would make no sense for there to be an absolute duty for everyone in society to commit suicide.
- **Suicide as moral pollution of society.** Augustine and Kant both express an ancient idea that suicide undermines the moral stability of society. Plato, for example, compared suicide to the cowardly soldier who quits the battlefield and Aristotle argued that someone who commits suicide has reduced the economic effectiveness of society. In other words both the citizen and society have a duty to each other to promote mutual welfare.
- **Suicide as violation of the principle to protect innocent life.** Aquinas in the natural law tradition argued that suicide is wrong because it undermines the principle that it is intrinsically wrong to kill an innocent life. This position reinforces many of the arguments made above and forms an important aspect of the debates today. Whereas we may argue for the right to life it does not follow that we also have a right to end our life. An innocent life is by definition no threat to society and must be protected.

Cross-reference

Hume's essay *Of Suicide* may be found in Peter Singer, *Applied Ethics*, Chapter II.

Key quote

Has not everyone of consequence, the free disposal of his own life.

DAVID HUME, *OF SUICIDE*

Key quote

Greater love has no man than this, that a man lay down his life for his friends.

GOSPEL OF JOHN 15:13

Moral arguments for suicide are:

- **Suicide as avoidance of unnecessary pain**. For hedonic utilitarians suicide is permissible if pain becomes so acute that it outweighs any other pleasures. There may be other considerations to take into account such as the effects on family and friends but there is nothing intrinsically wrong with suicide.
- **Suicide as exercise of autonomy**. David Hume's essay on suicide (1784) argues that suicide does not pollute society morally because 'A man who retires from life does no harm to society: he only ceases to do good.' In other words if someone decides not to contribute to society and he withdraws his labour, there is no contractual reason why society should stop him from taking his own life. Hume's argument reinforces the view that if I am the owner of my life then I have the right and autonomy to dispose of it as I wish. Hume's argument provides the basis for modern preference utilitarianism.
- **Suicide as virtue**. Altruistic suicide in particular illustrates that not all forms of suicide are the same. In the New Testament Jesus commends the person who lays down his life for his friends as the greatest act of love. Likewise in war we may commend the soldier who defends his comrades knowing he himself will be killed as a result.

3 The law on suicide and euthanasia

Until 1961 suicide in the UK was a criminal offence. Although the 1961 Suicide Act decriminalised suicide it *did not* make it morally licit. As the Suicide Act has direct consequences for euthanasia, it is worth noting its two major clauses:

a) 1961 Suicide Act

The Act states the following:

1. *The rule of law whereby it is a crime for a person to commit suicide is hereby abrogated.*
2. *(1) A person who aids, abets, counsels or procures the suicide of another or an attempt by another to commit suicide shall be liable for a term not exceeding fourteen years.*
   (2) If on the trial of an indictment for murder or manslaughter it is proved that the accused aided, abetted, counselled or procured the suicide of person in question, the jury may find him guilty of that offence.

Many think that law now supports the principle of autonomy. But, in fact, the Act reinforces the principle of sanctity of life by criminalising any form of assisted suicide. On the other hand the

Act does not hold the vitalist position that all life is equally valuable and should be preserved at all costs because there are cases when allowing a person to die is the better course of action.

b) The right to self determination

This distinction was famously illustrated in the **Diane Pretty** case in 2002. Diane Pretty, who was paralysed from the neck down with motor neurone disease, had asked her doctors to assist in her suicide. Her lawyers had presented the case based on the **right to self determination**. But her case was not upheld even when taken to the European Court of Human Rights. The reason given was that, although the law recognises the right to life, it does not consider its corollary is the right to die. Most importantly the courts decided that Mrs Pretty was not suffering from a life-threatening condition – if she *had* been, then doctors might have been able to argue that they could assist *in* her dying, even though they could not have helped in the direct *cause* of her death.

Key question

Although another ruling permitted the parents to make the final choice was it right to let Charlotte survive even though she is severely brain damaged and needs constant care?

On the other hand the case of **Baby Charlotte** in 2005, who was born prematurely and with severe brain damage, illustrates that the law does not consider life to be absolutely sacred. Against the wishes of her parents, the High Court ordered the doctors not to resuscitate the baby if she fell into a coma. The principle was that her underlying condition did not justify the medical assistance she was being given just to stay alive.

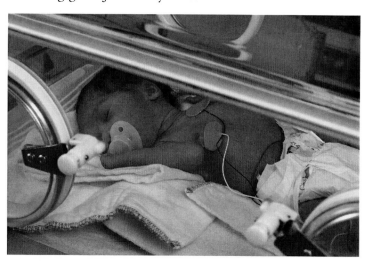

Who should decide if a sick premature baby should be allowed to die?

c) Physician aid in dying

Many consider that the law has led to considerable confusion and that one way of developing the present situation is to create a new Act which would permit **physician aid in dying**. The proposal states that there should be a bill to:

*Enable a competent adult who is suffering unbearably as a result of a
terminal illness to receive medical assistance to die at his own considered
and persistent request; and to make provision for a person suffering from
a terminal illness to receive pain relief medication.*

(Assisted Dying for the Terminally Ill Bill, 2004)

One of the major objections to proposals of this kind is the fear that
it will suffer from the **slippery slope** whereby what begins as
legitimate reasons to assist in a person's death will also permit non-
lethal conditions. This, it is claimed, will pollute society as Plato and
Augustine argued. In a letter to *The Times* (24 September 2004) a
group of eminent academic lawyers and philosophers, including
John Haldane and Alasdair MacIntyre, argued that:

- supporters of the Bill slide from making the condition one of
  actual unbearable suffering from terminal illness to merely the *fear*,
  discomfort and loss of dignity which terminal illness might bring;
- if quality of life is grounds for euthanasia for those who request it
  then logically this could be extended to those who don't request
  it (or who are unable to request it);
- the example in the Netherlands shows that the law cannot easily
  place safeguards against those who simply choose to ignore them.
  There is the difference between idea and practice in the 'real
  world'.

4 Allowing to die and cutting short a life

The problem of euthanasia is that it has to straddle both principle
and practicalities. Those who consider that there should not be a
right to terminate an innocent life nevertheless argue that there are
circumstances when some form of assisted dying is permissible. On
the other hand others consider this to be morally confusing and
argue that there are circumstances when 'cutting short' a life is not
only permissible but good.

Case study
Dr David Moor

His trial had concerned the death in 1997 of George Liddell,
an 85-year-old former ambulance worker who had recently
been discharged from hospital after treatment for bowel
cancer. He was bedridden, having suffered a stroke and a heart
attack, and was doubly incontinent, deaf, diabetic and anaemic.

The prosecution case hung upon a morphine injection Dr Moor gave to Mr Liddell on the morning of his death. When the investigation began, the doctor had not disclosed the injection to police or to NHS officials. He later gave details, saying that he had been panicked by media attention into withholding the information.

Outside the court, Dr Moor repeated his philosophy, saying: 'In caring for a terminally ill patient, a doctor is entitled to give pain-relieving medication which may have the incidental effect of hastening death. All I tried to do in treating Mr Liddell was to relieve his agony, distress and suffering. This has always been my approach in treating my patients with care and compassion. Doctors who treat dying patients to relieve their pain and suffering walk a tightrope to achieve this.' He insisted that the morphine he gave Mr Liddell was to relieve his pain and was in no way a lethal dose.

Detective Superintendent Colin Dobson of Northumbria Police said: 'To a police officer and the criminal justice system, the terms mercy killing and euthanasia are meaningless. If you shorten someone's life by minutes, that's murder, and by law we had to approach our investigation from this viewpoint.'

('Cheers as GP is cleared of murdering patient; Trial', *The Times*, 12 May 1999)

Dr Moor was acquitted of murder in 1999.

The Moor case illustrates the tension between those such as Dr Moor who argue that allowing to die is not the same as killing and those such as the detective who consider that there is either killing or not killing. The former position is largely supported by deontologists who support the **doctrine of double effect** and the second view by the consequential **utilitarians**.

a) Consequentialism: end and means

For most modern consequentialists all that matters in order to judge a situation is that the outcome is good or bad. Therefore an **omission**, such as failing to give a patient some drugs, is morally equivalent to giving a patient drugs if both actions have the effect of killing. Likewise some argue that a doctor who **refrains** from acting is no different from the one who acts if the intention (i.e. the desired outcome) is the same, just as in the same way the doctor who complies with a patient who **refuses** treatment directly assists in his suicide.

But is the consequentialist position entirely consistent?

Key quote

Thus an act or omission which, of itself or by intention, causes death in order to eliminate suffering constitutes a murder gravely contrary to the dignity of the human person and to the respect due to the living God, his Creator. The error of judgement into which one can fall in good faith does not change the nature of this murderous act, which must always be forbidden and excluded.

CATECHISM OF THE CATHOLIC CHURCH, PAGE 491

If A chooses to shoot B then we classify this as an intended act; if C sees A and fails to stop A shooting B then this is an intended omission. Is C at all **blameworthy**? C could claim that by not acting he was simply complying with another principle (e.g. never involve one's self in other people's affairs). Although the consequentialist claims to judge just the outcome, he does nevertheless assume that there are some significant non-consequential factors such as the duty of the doctor to be responsible for his patients.

b) Deontology: doctrine of double effect

A fairly typical expression of the doctrine of double effect is that a person may licitly perform an act which he foresees will produce good *and* evil if:

Key question

Does a person ever get to the stage where their life ceases to be worthwhile?

- the action in itself from the outset is good
- the good effect and not the evil is intended
- the good effect is not produced by means of the evil effect
- there is proportionately good reason to permit the evil effect.

So for example a consequentialist might argue that there is no moral difference between a patient who refuses treatment without a doctor and dies, than if a doctor is involved. The deontologist might well agree that in both cases the doctor is equally responsible but the quality of intention is far from trivial. For example there is a difference between the pacifist who refuses to fight on principle and the coward who fails to fight. The doctrine of double effect takes seriously the relationship established between the patient and doctor. Therefore refraining or acting in a patient's death is only permissible if the primary intention is *not* to kill even if this hastens death.

- **Purity of intention**. Consequentialists are unimpressed by the quality of intention argument. If the deontologist argues that he has foreseen a possible outcome then it does not matter how 'good' his intentions are or what kind of person he is: an evil act is an evil act. But the deontologist considers the quality of intention to be very important. There is a significant difference between the grandson who visits his grandmother because he has to and the one who does so because he wants to. In the latter case the outcome is enriched by **virtue** and, likewise, deceit can degrade an apparent act of kindness.
- **Arbitrariness**. Consequentialists object to the deontologist's distinction between intended foreseen effects and unintended foreseen effects. For example in the well-known example of the trolley bus, five people are lying on one track and one on another. At the moment the points are switched to the track with five people on it. For the utilitarian the choice is simple, change the points and save the five. But the deontologist argues that life is not that simple. For example if I have one healthy person and five sick

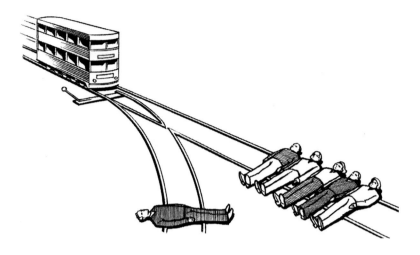

Should the train be allowed to carry on in its course to kill five people?

people and I could use the organs of the healthy person to cure the five, do I have a duty to sacrifice the one? The deontologist argues that it is logically possible to have *prior* intentions – I could refrain and allow the trolley bus to kill five people on the grounds that it would be more evil *intentionally* to kill one person. But for most consequentialists this defence is irrational and arbitrary.

- **Ordinary and extraordinary means.** Consequentialists consider that the deontologist's rigid refusal ever to use direct killing can lead to more suffering, loss of dignity and confusion over exactly what constitutes 'extraordinary' means. For example in the natural law tradition a person who refuses food and water in order to die has deliberately committed suicide which is condemned in Roman Catholic theology as a mortal sin. But a person is within their rights to refuse surgery on the grounds that it is over and above what is needed ordinarily for basic existence.

- **Proportionality and quality of life.** The consequentialists point out that the final element of the double effect includes the consequential principle that the evil of the unintended action must not be greater than the intended one. In other words if prolonging life would bring about disproportionate suffering, then the deontologist should surely permit direct killing. The use of QALYs or 'quality adjusted life years' in some hospitals is thought to be an **empirical** means of determining the quality of life of a patient in terms of the resources needed to maintain a life. Deontologists agree that outcomes are important but argue that the consequentialist underestimates the importance of means and the very subjective nature of a QALY; namely who decides what constitutes a worthwhile life?

5 Non-voluntary euthanasia

In non-voluntary euthanasia a decision is made on behalf of the patient on the strength of the situation. The landmark case of **Tony Bland** in the UK was after the Hillsborough football disaster in April 1989. Bland was placed on a life-support and although able to feed and breathe was in a deep coma. Finally after lengthy legal debate his life-support was turned off. The significance of the case is that it acknowledged that doctors cannot be expected to maintain a life (however defined) at all costs. The moral issue is whether prolonging the life of 'brain dead' patients is in their best interests.

a) PVS and the problem of defining death

The Bland case and others like it have set a precedent which has significantly shifted not only how we understand death but the value of life as well. In the past death was defined as when the heart ceased pumping blood round the body accompanied with the cessation of other vital bodily functions. Today, a person can be kept 'alive' in this sense for long periods of time even though, as in the Bland case, important parts of the brain have ceased to operate. Being 'pink and supple' does not necessarily equate with being alive. Coma patients in this state can perform a number of involuntary actions and contrary to what many people think the patient is not necessarily lying inert in bed. The new definition of death is when there is no brain activity. So, a patient who is in a **persistent vegetative state** (PVS) where they have lost part of the brain (i.e. the cerebral cortex) would theoretically be deemed dead even if his body was functioning. But recent research has revealed how difficult making such a diagnosis is. Not only can it take some time to determine whether the patient is indeed brain dead but it is now apparent that the brain can function at very low levels, just enough to provide vital hormones for the body.

b) Deciding on the patient's best interests

In practice being in a PVS or being declared 'brain dead' is not always taken to mean that the patient is dead (if that were the case then there would be no debate). The issue in broad terms is whether sustaining him on life-support is in their best interests. In other words, 'life' is not just a biological fact but also a moral or evaluative judgement. The same problem of defining death and balancing it against the best interests of a patient also occurs when taking organs from a dead patient. The **dead donor rule** is used by some to define death as both lack of brain and body function. This rules out any form of euthanasia.

Perhaps in the end each case has to be viewed separately on its own merits.

Key question

When does a human being cease to be a person? Consider again the problems of personhood on pages 18–21.

Key quote

The ability to make complex judgements about benefit requires compassion, experience and an appreciation of the patient's viewpoint.

THE BRITISH MEDICAL ASSOCIATION
(*MEDICAL ETHICS TODAY*, PAGE 170)
ABOUT TREATMENT OF PVS PATIENTS

Cross-reference

Read page 118 below on the dead donor rule and problems of defining death.

6 Virtues and euthanasia

Key question

Which virtues are particularly important when dealing with the terminally ill?

In Chapter 1 we noted Beauchamp's and Childress' principles for a code for doctors and health care workers. We have seen the problem that doctors have of balancing rules and consequences when making end of life decisions. We have also noted the complexity of working within the professional medical ethical tradition of the four principles: respect for **autonomy** (freedom to exercise one's will), **non-maleficence** (avoiding harm), **beneficence** (producing benefits) and **justice** (distributing benefits, risks and costs fairly).

But as Beauchamp and Childress note, perhaps the most important consideration which binds all these factors together is the character of the doctor or physician who has to treat and care for his patients.

A patient–doctor relationship depends on trust, but does trust inform the right to life or the right to choose? Unless the virtue ethicist clarifies which ethical system he is working with, this cannot be decided. On the other hand, some would argue that a duty of care to a patient is not to keep them alive at all costs; euthanasia or allowing to die could be good medicine. 'Thou shalt not kill; but need'st not strive officiously to keep alive' (Arthur Clough) is often quoted as an example of avoiding the extreme of excess (such as officiousness or keeping alive at all costs) and deficiency (such as cowardice through inaction and allowing to die). The quotation illustrates that, although doctors have a prima facie duty of beneficence, without the **corresponding virtue** of benevolence or compassion it becomes impossible to know how to make beneficence work properly in practice. Virtues therefore *enhance* the quality of care given to a patient on an individual basis and *enable* the doctor to balance consequences with his professional duties in every situation.

Summary diagram

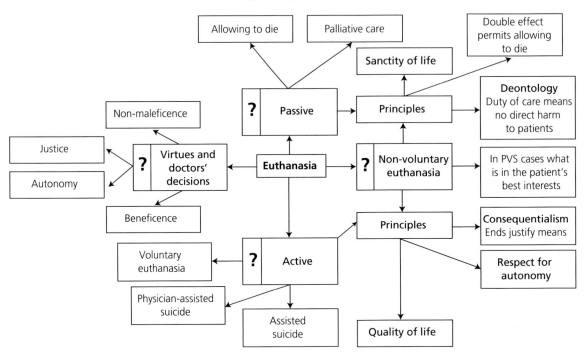

Study guide

By the end of this chapter you should have considered the problems of trying to define the moral (and legal) distinctions between different types of suicide and euthanasia. You should be clear about the ambiguities between passive and active euthanasia and the significance of these distinctions for doctors and their patients. Finally, you should be aware of the debate between the consequentialists and the deontologists when dealing with euthanasia and care for the dying.

Revision checklist

Can you explain the view of suicide as stated by each of the following:

■ Plato, Aristotle, Augustine, Aquinas, Hume and Kant.

Can you explain the moral difference between:

■ allowing to die and cutting short a life from a consequential position
■ allowing to die and cutting short a life from a deontological position.

Can you explain the difference between:

- suicide, physician-aided suicide, aid in dying, voluntary euthanasia, passive euthanasia and non-voluntary euthanasia.

Do you know:

- what the 1961 Suicide Act states
- the law on voluntary euthanasia.

Can you give arguments for and against:

- palliative care when dealing with the very sick and dying
- allowing very premature babies to die
- the use of virtue ethics for doctors in their treatment of the terminally ill.

Essay question

1a. Explain what is meant by a quality of life argument.

1b. 'Palliative care for the dying is preferable to euthanasia.' Discuss.

To demonstrate knowledge and understanding you should begin by stating how and why quality of life arguments reject sanctity of life arguments. Quality of life arguments should be shown to have a view of humans in terms of what preferences or desires have to be fulfilled in order to say that a life is worthwhile. This can be done by referring to any form of utilitarianism and in particular to Peter Singer's preference utilitarianism.

The evaluation should centre on the issue of whether it is right deliberately to cut short a life through euthanasia or to offer nursing and care to reduce suffering but to refrain from direct killing. The analysis will have to focus on intentions and whether, if the outcomes are similar (i.e. the eventual death of a dying patient), choosing not to kill a patient might cause more suffering or whether the rule never to cause direct harm to a patient must be maintained to ensure the principle of non-maleficence.

Further essay questions

2a Explain how revealed ethics might be applied to the issue of euthanasia.

2b 'Euthanasia should never be permitted in any circumstance.' Discuss.

3 'Allowing a terminally ill patient to die cannot be morally wrong.' Discuss.

4 Assess the view that euthanasia is always contrary to good medical practice.

Chapter checklist

This chapter considers what a right is and whether a woman or couple have a right to a child. Natural rights and human rights are distinguished. The argument that a child is a gift not a right is supported by sanctity of life arguments. The causes of infertility are reviewed. One solution is surrogacy but this raises issues of the rights of the surrogate and commissioning parents. Normative ethical responses to surrogacy are reviewed. The second part of the chapter looks at IVF (*in vitro* fertilisation) and the use and rights of donor egg/sperm and frozen embryos. Normative ethical responses to IVF are reviewed.

1 Infertility and the right to a child

a) Right to a child

Before we can answer the question whether a couple have a right to a child we have first to consider what rights are. There are no simple answers to this. Rights theorists today generally distinguish between **natural rights** and **human rights**. Natural rights are those rights which can be discerned through natural law. **John Locke** (1632–1704) was the first to set out clearly what this means. Natural rights are endowed by God in nature to ensure that all human beings do not harm each other's lives, health, liberty and possessions. Equally therefore everyone has a *duty* not to harm the lives, liberty and possessions of others. Most importantly Locke argued that rights are there to protect people against the intrusive power of governments and authorities.

On the other hand **Jeremy Bentham** (1748–1832) and others dismissed natural law and with it natural rights because there is no rational evidence for their existence. Legal or human rights, he argued, are developed by society and are facts in so far as we can give a rational reason for their existence.

But the problem with Bentham's view is that if a definition of a right is that it is a universal entitlement to all human beings, then they can't be merely the legal rights developed by a particular

Key question

What are rights? How are they to be decided?

society or culture. So, rights do appear to have some kind of 'natural' basis, whatever type of rights is being suggested. All appear to assume that being human is sufficient to demand certain basic human entitlements and in addition these rights protect individuals against the intrusive power of governments.

Rights theorists often consider that there are three levels or generations of rights:

1 **Basic freedoms** and protection from the abuse of power from others.
2 **Socio-economic goods** and services from a welfare state: education, security, medicine, etc.
2 **Collective goods** such as rights to economic social development, peace, healthy environment, etc.

All rights therefore assume something about the nature of being human. But what are these? Suggestions include:

- worth due to persons
- basic human needs
- human agency and autonomy
- self ownership.

So which of these various rights theories might support the view that a woman or a couple have a universal right to a child? Article 16 of the *Universal Declaration of Human Rights* states, 'Men and women of full age...have the right to marry and found a family.'

Key quotes

Men and women of full age...have the right to marry and found a family.

UNIVERSAL DELCARATION OF
HUMAN RIGHTS, ARTICLE 16

Over himself, over his own body and mind, the individual is sovereign.

JS MILL, *ON LIBERTY*

But Article 16 is ambiguous. It might be argued that it merely states in negative terms that no one should hinder a couple from marrying and having a child if they wish. It doesn't make it an entitlement to have a child as a matter of human rights. If it did then it would be a duty of the state to provide the means for those who are infertile to have a child, on the grounds of basic human needs.

Some, therefore, have argued for the right based on self ownership. If, as Mill famously stated, 'Over himself, over his own body and mind, the individual is sovereign' (*On Liberty*) then a woman, at least, has the right to exercise the full potential of her body to have a child as a 'worth due' to her as a woman. But even if this could be demonstrated does it necessarily follow that she also has a 'welfare right' to demand of the state the medical aid to have a child if she is infertile?

More controversial is whether a homosexual or lesbian couple have a right to a child in order to form a family. Article 16 doesn't accommodate gay marriage, but in many parts of the world this has now been accepted. If this is accepted, the same arguments for a right to a child could be applied.

Key question

Does a child have a right to a mother and father?

b) Children as a gift

Despite the benefits of assisted reproduction, there are many who argue that these technologies have wrongly suggested that every couple has a right to a child. This view is most clearly stated by the Roman Catholic Church. Both natural law and biblical revealed law teach that children should be born within marriage and as the result of sexual intercourse. Children may be the 'blessing' of marriage as a gift (e.g. Genesis 4:1, Psalm 127:3) but not a right.

But there is disagreement whether an infertile couple may use assisted reproduction. Some argue that infertility may be treated like any other illness, but others draw the line once any treatment is used which separates the unitive and procreative purpose of sex. The Roman Catholic Church therefore counsels sterile or infertile couples to channel their energies into other creative acts such as 'adoption, various forms of educational work and assistance to other families and to the poor or handicapped children' (*On Respect for Life*).

c) Infertility

Infertility is a broad term. Anthony Dyson (*The Ethics of IVF*, page 11) outlines the four stages of the reproduction process where a pregnancy may fail:

1 failure to find adequate sperm or eggs
2 failure to conceive (egg and sperm do not meet)
3 the fertilised gamete fails to implant into the lining of the uterus
4 repeated failure of early pregnancies.

Between 10 and 15 per cent of couples are infertile in the West. More precisely this means that, whereas 90 per cent of couples may *conceive* in the first year and 96 per cent in the second year of trying for a child, around 45 per cent of women miscarry without knowing. Women account for some 50 to 70 per cent of all infertility, men between 20 and 30 per cent of all infertility.

Infertility, for whatever reason, is the cause of considerable anguish, as this husband recounts:

> *If I cannot give my wife the baby she wants, I do not have anything worthy of giving to anyone I love... My wife and I have come to a resolution of our infertility as a couple. We are the adoptive parents of a fine girl who thrives and finds our love... I accept my infertility, but I will never, fully, be reconciled to it.*
>
> (quoted in A. Dyson, *The Ethics of IVF*, page 13)

Is infertility better considered as a health issue or just an unfortunate state of affairs? In either case, should it be treated through public health care?

- Infertility is an illness or disease like many others which may afflict otherwise healthy people. It can therefore be treated.
- If infertility is considered a malfunction or aberration of nature, then the use of technology may help rectify the fault and put the process back on its natural course.

d) Technology and patriarchy

Key question

Does reproductive technology liberate or oppress women?

Many feminists warn that reproductive technologies represent an unacceptable level of intrusion into a woman's life. IVF, in particular, necessitates a long series of hormone treatment, extraction of eggs, and surgical operations. It is physically and emotionally draining and expensive. But the chief objection is that it removes the control a woman has over her own body; technology is a form of patriarchy exercising its power over her body, manipulating it to reproduce. For some, thinking in Marxist terms, it is an example of an oppressive society where the means of production or rather reproduction have been obliquely removed from women. By using technology controlled by men, it has allowed an external power to interfere and manipulate at every stage. So, whereas some feminists have seen the reproductive technological revolution as the great liberation (donor insemination for instance can liberate her from the demands of a genetic father, or in some cases from a male relationship altogether), others have been far more hesitant.

In her novel *The Handmaid's Tale* (1985), the feminist novelist Margaret Atwood invents a future dystopia where reproductive technology has turned tail, reducing women to their various sexual functions. There are Marthas who clean and cook; Jezebels or prostitutes who provide for pleasure; Handmaids or reproductive prostitutes; Wives or infertile women who act as social secretaries. The whole system is geared so that men can control the right conditions to have perfect offspring divorced from love and affection. Women and children have become no more than commodities and producers. Atwood's message clearly warns women against the unthinking use of technology which can unwittingly become another form of patriarchy and exploitation of women.

2 Surrogacy

Surrogacy is a general term used to describe the situation where a woman bears a child for another couple. Some dispute whether 'surrogacy' is an appropriate term. The 'host' or surrogate mother undergoes all the emotions and psychological changes that accompany a pregnancy and it is these experiences which have to be taken into account. If it were possible to hire an incubator or lease a womb independently of the person, then there would be no sense in which the machine or disembodied womb could be considered a mother. But the surrogate is not a machine and in many legal systems the person who bears a child is the mother, whether or not she is genetically related to the child.

The central moral problems of surrogacy are:

- the legal status of surrogacy contracts
- the rights of the surrogate and intended parents
- the physical and mental risks
- the nature of motherhood.

a) The law and surrogacy

Surrogacy poses questions about what is meant by being a parent. This can be seen in the range of terms used:

- **Commissioning or intended parents** are those who initiate or commission the surrogacy and bring the child up as their own.
- **Genetic parents** are those who provide sperm and egg.
- **Surrogate mother** or host mother who bears the child. It is an ambiguous term. If for instance the 'surrogate' provides genetic material she is also the **'biological mother'** and the social mother is strictly the surrogate. Legally the surrogate mother is the child's mother, not the intended mother.

The issues are further complicated by the type of surrogacy used:

- **Partial surrogacy** occurs when the surrogate or host mother provides her egg which is fertilised either *in vitro* and placed through artificial insemination into the womb or she is artificially inseminated by the intended father's sperm. Only in very rare cases would sexual intercourse take place.
- **Full surrogacy** occurs when the intended parents provide egg and sperm. In some cases a donor (either egg or sperm) may be used. The surrogate or host mother therefore has no genetic links to the baby. The fertilised gamete is placed into the host mother's womb.
- **Commercial surrogacy** refers to arrangements whereby a woman is contracted and paid to be a surrogate mother and to deliver a baby to the intended parents. In many countries commercial surrogacy is illegal.
- **Voluntary or altruistic surrogacy** refers to a surrogacy arrangement where the surrogate mother voluntarily offers to bear a child for another couple but not for commercial gain. Her motives could be out of love (a sister's love for her sister or brother), charity (a Christian concern for a childless couple to have a family) or self-fulfilment (the sensation of having a baby).

1985 Surrogacy Act: it is illegal to arrange, agree about or take part in a commercial surrogacy arrangement. Voluntary surrogacy is not illegal because there is no financial gain. Payment is considered to have taken place if there is the involvement of a third party (such as an agency) or if the surrogate expects a payment to be made. It is also illegal to advertise for a surrogate mother or intended parents. Reasonable payment for loss of earnings, treatments costs, child care etc. are permitted. COTS (the voluntary surrogacy charity in the UK) suggest that intended parents should budget for up to £12,000 (2007).

The **Human Fertilisation and Embryology Act** (1990) amended the 1985 Act so that surrogacy arrangements cannot be enforced by law and either party can change its mind at any time. The intended parents may become the legal parents of the child, but until that time the child is legally the surrogate mother's and, if she is married or has a partner, he is the legal father – unless it can be shown that he has not consented to the procedure. A **parental order** must be arranged six weeks after and within six months of the birth of the child (even if both intended parents are also the genetic parents). The child must be living with the intended parents in the UK. The intended parents must be over 18 and married. The surrogate mother must be in agreement. The birth certificate will be altered, but at 18 the child will be able to obtain a copy of the original certificate which will contain the name of the surrogate mother.

If the surrogate has supplied her egg to be fertilised she is to be treated as a donor and the same screening procedures (controlled by the licensing authority) apply to her as with any donor.

Key word

A **parental order** is equivalent to adoption but quicker. It can be obtained by applying to the courts.

Case study
The case of 'Baby M'

The case of 'Baby M' (as it was referred to in the courts) is significant because of the legislation which took place afterwards concerning surrogacy contracts and also because of the continued moral issues which it raises.

The essential facts of the case are as follows (Gregory Pence, *Classic Cases in Medical Ethics*, pages 121–132):

- Elizabeth and William Stern are both well educated and well-to-do physicians living in New Jersey (USA).
- Elizabeth thought she should not have a child as she claimed to have the symptoms of multiple sclerosis and having a baby would exacerbate the condition.

- In 1985 they chose Mary Beth Whitehead (married to Richard) to be a surrogate because she looked similar to Elizabeth. Both the Whiteheads are lower income earners and he is an alcoholic. The surrogacy is commercial (she agreed to the $10,000 contract) and partial (she provided the egg and William Stern the sperm). Richard initially had misgivings.

- However, during the pregnancy she thinks of the baby as 'hers'. She fails at first to have an amniocentesis test despite the condition of the contract. Later she does and learns of the sex of the foetus. She fails to divulge the information to the Sterns.

- Mary Beth tells her own children that she doesn't want to 'sell their sister'.

- Reluctantly, just before the birth she signs the paternity papers giving the baby to the Sterns.

- Baby M is born 27th March 1986. Richard is registered by Mary Beth as the father. First, Mary Beth allows the Sterns to have the baby then says she feels suicidal at the thought of giving up the baby and the Sterns allow her to take the baby home for a week. Then she refuses to give up the baby and the baby is hidden.

- The Sterns take the case to court.

- Mary Beth falls ill and whilst she is in hospital the baby is found and returned to the Sterns to look after as a temporary custody measure.

- At the trial in January 1987 the case centred on Mary Beth's character. She was considered to be a liar and had accused William Stern of sexually abusing her own children. The judge concluded that commercial surrogacy contracts were not illegal and the baby should legally be considered to belong to the Sterns. The judge was accused of bias. Many feminists supported Mary Beth: 'A one night stand in a dish doesn't make a man a father' and that surrogacy was a form of 'reproductive prostitution'.

- On 3rd February 1988 the New Jersey Supreme Court on appeal reversed the initial decision and ruled that surrogacy contracts were illegal and constituted a form of baby selling. The Sterns were allowed to keep the baby but Elizabeth Stern could not adopt her and Mary Beth's status was confirmed as the legal and natural mother.

b) Rights of surrogate and commissioning parents

i) Motherhood

Key question

Is a mother the person who gives birth to a child or the person who looks after it?

The issue of surrogacy questions what it means to be a mother. Is it necessary for a child to have a mother who is genetically related to him or her? There is no consistent answer here. On the one hand, as in the case of 'Baby M', many feminist groups argued that Mary Beth, the surrogate, should be considered the real mother – she had after all not only provided the genetic material but *nurtured* the child from conception. Motherhood might then be considered to be more than simply providing an egg, but the intimate, psychological, possibly spiritual, process of giving the foetus/baby its first formative experiences. Supposing, though, Baby M had been conceived using full surrogacy, would the complete lack of genetic contribution by Mary Beth have made any difference to the motherhood argument?

ii) Rights of the surrogate and intended parents

Key question

Does a surrogate mother have any rights over the child she gives birth to?

Surrogacy is characterised by the contract between the intended parents and the surrogate or host mother who will bear the child. The necessity of a contract from the beginning suggests an ambiguity about the ownership, rights and responsibilities towards the child.

Mary Beth's contract had stipulated that she should have an amniocentesis. An amniocentesis establishes early on in the pregnancy whether the foetus is suffering from any abnormality (Down's Syndrome for instance). Supposing the foetus is thought to be deformed, the question is whether an abortion contrary to the wishes of the surrogate is legally binding.

In the situation of voluntary surrogacy does the surrogate mother have the right to an abortion (she does not want to give the intended parents a 'damaged' child) even if that is contrary to the wishes of the intended parents? There is some ambiguity about who owns the unborn child. As far as the law is concerned in Britain (see above) the surrogate mother is the legal mother until she consents to hand over the baby to the intended parents.

iii) Commercialism and slavery

Many **feminists** argue that surrogacy represents some of the worst aspects of capitalist societies. In Marxist terms women are classed according to their reproductive functions – even by other women: rich women hire poor women to meet their reproductive needs. The result is reminiscent of black slavery in America where the slaves were judged according to their effectiveness. Women equally might be judged according to whether they are child begetters, childbearers and child rearers.

In the 'Baby M' case many argued that Mary Beth's rights as a mother were violated because of her poverty. She had been forced into selling her baby because of wider social conditions which had prevented her from exercising her rights. Commercial surrogacy has therefore been resisted by many countries not only because it is a form of **slavery** (by selling the child) but also a trap which exploits poor women and a loophole for unscrupulous business people.

Some philosophers have argued that even had Mary Beth been paid *more* she would still have been exploited; the money would have become an even more *coercive* incentive to give up her maternal rights. It was for this reason that some feminists at the time regarded Mary Beth's case as a form of 'commercial prostitution' and a further denigration of women.

Finally surrogacy exploits the stereotype that considers that women as carers ought to be compassionate. Surrogacy puts emotional pressure on women to be compassionate (perhaps for a childless sister or friend). As no such obligation applies to men, women should be free equally from such decisions.

iv) Autonomy and solidarity

For many feminists women may use whatever reproductive technologies they wish. If a woman is hindered from using her reproductive capacity this is hardly recognition of her freedom to choose. Furthermore, surrogacy can unite the infertile woman and the surrogate woman in an act of solidarity. It can reduce the superiority some women feel over others who can reproduce and those who cannot; surrogacy might even provide a new paradigm or model in the West for collaborative reproduction *and* parenting. The role of a proper legally binding contract could ensure that the confusions and misunderstandings (as illustrated in the 'Baby M' case) be kept to a minimum.

c) Normative ethical responses to surrogacy

i) Natural law

If infertility is considered a malfunction or aberration of nature, then is it necessarily wrong to use technology to rectify the fault? In general, natural ethicists are against surrogacy for the following reasons:

- The proper purpose or *telos* of sexual intercourse is a child. When a couple have sex this must be their primary intention. If they are unable to procreate they must accept this.
- Those who use surrogates and gamete donors threaten the institution of marriage and family. Surrogacy destroys the narrative coherency of parenting from the **unitive** act of sex to birth to the rearing of the child.

Key thought

Slavery occurs when a person is owned by another as their property. As property they can be sold and traded to another person. Slavery is against Article 4 of the Universal Declaration of Human Rights, 'No one shall be held in slavery or servitude; slavery and the slave trade shall be prohibited in all their forms.'

Key quote

Surrogacy is an insult both to the surrogate and to the child.

AGNETA SUTTON, *INFERTILITY*, PAGE 43

Key word

The **unitive** aspect to sexual intercourse describes both the physical act itself and the psychological dimension of love.

- Children need to feel part of the narrative coherency. A child needs to be able to know who his or her genetic parents are if only to make sense of his or her own identity.
- The involvement of a surrogate is worse than the use of a donor gamete because it is psychologically more intrusive. It might cause psychological or spiritual confusion to the natural order of marriage. The intended father might naturally feel that the surrogate is the real mother of his baby rather than his wife. It is in effect **adultery**.
- Surrogacy might encourage gay couples to have children. As homosexuality can never be procreative, surrogacy destroys the unitive/procreative purpose of sex and cannot be permitted.

ii) Kantian ethics

Key question

Does surrogacy depersonalise the child into a thing?

Key quote

Kant's practical imperative: *'Act in such a way that you treat humanity, whether in your own person or in the person of another, always at the same time as an end never simply as a means.'*

Many find the commercialisation of pregnancy deeply repugnant. It reduces human relationships to the market place and turns the baby into a commodity and the mother into a service industry. These are the views expressed by Kant's second version of the categorical imperative, the practical imperative, which is never to treat people as a means to an end but an end in themselves. Modern Kantian philosophers have generally argued against surrogacy for the following reasons:

- Every person is as valuable as anyone else; we all have an absolute duty to respect all persons, unconditionally.
- Treating the surrogate as a means to an end reduces her freedom and well-being.
- The autonomy and well-being of the commissioning parents is also severely reduced; as they are driven by the overwhelming desire for a child, they are not acting according to reason.
- Desire for a child depersonalises the baby into a desired 'thing' or commodity.
- A surrogacy contract or agreement depersonalises the commissioning parents. A contract which stipulates what the surrogate can/cannot eat, whether she may have sex, whether she may abort or not abort (in the case of handicap) etc. turns a relationship into a process which is demeaning to all concerned.

But Kantians are most critical of surrogates themselves:

- The surrogate reduces herself to an object and, far from acting in an autonomous rational way, she is motivated by money, or the 'image' of being a giver or 'martyr'.
- She is satisfying her own inclinations and selling services that should really be the duty of a husband or spouse.

Key quote

The basic moral case for contract law, indeed for capitalism itself, rests on the voluntary nature of exchange. Commercial trade is good for all parties involved, or else they wouldn't engage in it. And in the vast majority of commercial transactions – including the vast majority of surrogate-motherhood contracts – the deal goes through with no problem, suggesting that both parties do indeed consider themselves better off.

MICHAEL KINSLEY QUOTED IN PENCE, *CLASSIC CASES IN MEDICAL ETHICS*, PAGE 139

Key question

What are the qualities of a good parent?

- Effectively, what she is doing is a form of prostitution. For example in the case of 'Baby M', Mary Beth went through the whole process of a mothering experiencing which could never fully be satisfied because she could never be fully involved in the upbringing of the child.
- The surrogate treats the baby as a means to an end and by doing so she has forfeited her autonomy by acting for a particular couple. Acting as a surrogate is inconsistent with the idea of what it means to be a mother; it cannot be a universal duty of all women to act in this way.

But many find the Kantian perspective puzzling. Surrogacy doesn't reduce autonomy if each person fully understands their commitments. From a liberal perspective surrogacy offers another option to childless couples and allows women who wish to be surrogates the ability to use their reproductive capabilities for charitable ends. Acting generously to others is not contrary to Kant's kingdom of ends which encourages selfless actions for others.

iii) Virtue ethics

Whilst the virtue ethicist might not comment directly on whether surrogacy should or should not take place, he can help to reflect on some of the principles. One central issue the virtue ethicist might consider is what constitutes the **good parent**.

From an instrumentalist utilitarian position the answer to this question might be: the good parent is one who can feed and nurture the child, and offer a stable environment for the child to grow and flourish. The law only offers a minimum requirement that the commissioning parents are married. Even this is contentious as many gay or lesbian couples consider that they can be good parents if they are living in a stable, loving relationship. In other words, virtue ethicists might argue that the instrumental principle of 'the good parent' is not sufficient unless matched by qualities which society generally considers are necessary for all healthy relationships.

- In 2005 a Leeds couple, Mr and Mrs J, entered into a surrogacy agreement with a woman and her husband, Mr and Mrs P, from Bristol.
- But although Mrs P had made an agreement to hand over the child at birth to Mr J (the natural father) she had refused to do so. Court proceedings followed.
- In July 2007 the Court of Appeal of the three judges ruled that Mr and Mrs J would make 'better parents'.

- The judgement was based on the fact that Mrs P had never intended to hand over the baby and actively deceived Mr and Mrs J from the start.
- There was no doubt that materially the baby had not suffered, but from a virtue ethical point of view Mrs P's obsessive character and her inability to balance her needs with those of the child's and commissioning parents suggest that she had none of the characteristics which would make her a good parent in the future.

The ruling is significant because under surrogacy law Mrs P and her husband are the legal parents, yet the judges' apparent use of a virtue demonstrates that strict application of principles alone must not be blind to the human aspect of the situation.

Nevertheless the decision begs the question. If the law can interfere here (and in adoption cases) and decide what constitutes a good parent, what stops it doing so in ordinary circumstances – any couple can have a child whatever their politics, racial mix or social behaviour, whereas those wishing to adopt have to pass rigorous interviews to show that they will be 'good parents'.

Perhaps for consistency *all* potential parents should be screened before they start a family. But besides the impracticalities, such a gross invasion into personal liberties would undermine the fundamentals of a liberal democracy.

However, the cases are not entirely parallel; it is because surrogacy is an *artificial* process involving a form of public contract that the law is able to impose some regulations for the general good which might well entail determining what constitutes a good parent.

iv) Utilitarianism

Key question

What are the psychological and physical risks of surrogacy?

Almost any utilitarian system sets out a calculus which weighs up the risks against the benefits of surrogacy.

Utilitarian risks/harm:

- physical problems incurred in all pregnancies (e.g. nausea, miscarriage, threat to life, etc.);
- the surrogate bonds with the child causing trauma when having to give up the baby;
- having to be a parent in a way they didn't intend, as expected by the commissioning parents;
- commissioning parents might be blackmailed by the surrogate for more attention, money, etc.;
- psychological harm to the child caused by having several types of parent;
- physical harm to the unborn child if the surrogate doesn't eat properly, etc.;
- rejection by surrogate/intended parents if the child is handicapped or just not wanted.

Utilitarian benefits:

- allows women who wish to sell their reproductive services to do so;
- happiness at being able to give the gift of life to an infertile couple;
- the joy of the commissioning parents of having a child;
- as a collaborate effort many people can benefit.

For the **rule utilitarians** the thorny area of surrogate agreements/contracts is especially important. Contracts can certainly help to reduce misunderstanding and confusion and minimise the potential harms. **Feminist utilitarians** argue that the law could recognise the surrogate as providing a useful role in society and protect her by law. In the past many women have had key roles in the rearing of other people's children (nannies, wet nurses, etc.) but they had no legal rights.

But even utilitarians might ask whether there is something fundamentally harmful about surrogacy. G.E. Moore's 'open question' prompts the question 'But is it good?' The **ideal utilitarian** might question, as the Kantians do, whether treating human life in this way is good. It is dubious whether organ selling or womb leasing can ever be an entirely rational act. As Mary Beth's lawyer Harold Cassidy said after the end of her trial, surrogate mothers 'cannot know, until after the child is born, their true feelings about bearing that child'. There is equally no way of judging the long-term psychological effects on the child. The question of **long-term consequences** remains problematic especially for the **welfare utilitarian**. The question for the welfare utilitarian is whether society is better off with surrogacy or without it.

v) Revealed ethics

Many Christians consider surrogacy (both commercial and voluntary) to violate the view that life cannot be owned by anyone. The principles of the **sanctity of life** suggest that life is a gift from God (Genesis 1:27, Job 1:21) and that humans do not own it but rather act as its stewards and nurture it. Some **liberal Christians** argue that offering to be a surrogate exemplifies the principle of love or agape. Her act is sacrificial and generous and enables a couple to have a family, which is one of the purposes of marriage. However, many are less sure that surrogacy in practice really achieves this idealistic end.

A good starting point for Christian discussion is the Old Testament story of Abraham, Sarah and Hagar (Genesis 16:1–12).

> ### Key quote
>
> *The practical and moral problems are multiple and involve a confused complexity of relationships which we do not believe it is possible to resolve at present.*
>
> CHURCH OF ENGLAND REPORT, *PERSONAL ORIGINS*, PAGE 59

- The story relates that when Abraham finds that Sarah is barren he takes Hagar, one of his serving girls, and makes her his concubine – effectively his surrogate. Their child is Ishmael.
- When eventually Sarah does bears Abraham's child, Isaac, one of her first acts is to banish Hagar and Ishmael from their home.
- Ishmael loses his rights of inheritance.
- Sarah's jealousy and Abraham's feebleness capture the psychological problems associated with surrogacy.

For many **black Christian feminists** the story of Hagar illustrates the ways in which women have frequently been slaves to a triple jeopardy of sex, race and poverty. As soon as she becomes a concubine she even loses the rights of a slave and she and Ishmael are treated not as people but as property to be disposed of.

Feminist Christians share the same views as many non-Christian feminists that for some people today children are status symbols. Sarah without a child had far less power than when she eventually had her own child. Surrogacy exacerbates the situation by commercialising and objectifying the process (as Kantians also suggest). Many sad examples today illustrate how some commissioning parents don't feel the same degree of obligation to children they haven't been part of from the start. And finally does the commercial metaphor also suggest that if the commissioning parents are not entirely happy with the 'product' (i.e. the child) or if the product is damaged can it be returned to the surrogate? The writers of the Church of England's report on assisted reproduction come to a similar conclusion:

> *The practical and moral problems are multiple and involve a confused complexity of relationships which we do not believe it is possible to resolve at present. Strong bonding, for example, takes place between a woman and the child she bears in her womb and this may lead her being unwilling to let the child go to the contracting couple after birth.*
>
> (*Personal Origins*, page 59)

Summary diagram

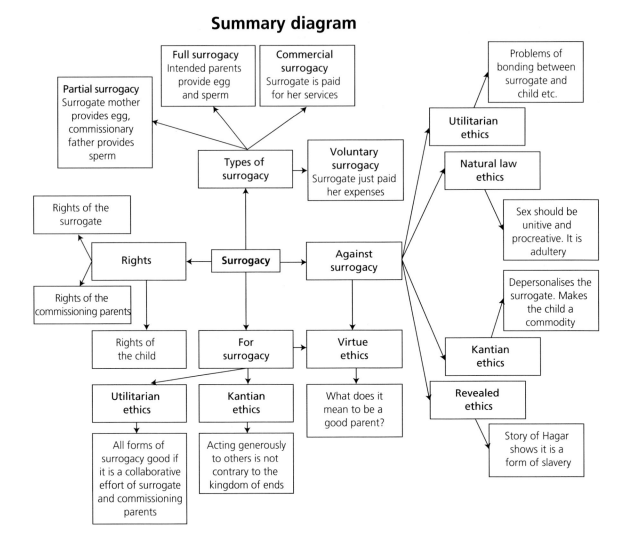

3 *In vitro* fertilisation

Key question

At what point does the use of reproductive technology become unacceptable?

In vitro fertilisation or IVF covers a range of artificial reproductive processes. As a reproductive technology it not only enables childless couples to form families as close to the natural process as possible, but also ensures that future children can be screened and genetic abnormalities removed.

Many of the arguments for and against IVF are already covered by surrogacy but because IVF deals with the actual process of conception it poses some very particular ethical questions. Some of these ethical questions are:

- Is it right to use donor gametes?
- Is it right to create a life if it is then to be destroyed?

- Is it permissible to carry out experiments on embryos?
- Is it right to produce human life separately from the physical, unitive act of sexual intercourse?

a) The law and infertility methods

The law which controls the processes is the **Human Fertilisation and Embryology Act** (1990). The Act also made provision for the founding of the **Human Fertilisation and Embryology Authority (HFEA)** which is authorised to oversee the provisions of the Act.

IVF technologies serve three purposes. Firstly, to help overcome male and female infertility, secondly, to screen against genetic abnormalities and, thirdly, to provide the opportunity for research into infertility and other human genetic disorders.

- *In vitro* **fertilisation or IVF**. The egg and sperm are fertilised outside the womb 'in glass' (i.e. *in vitro*) or a petri dish, and then at the two-to-eight cell stage transferred to the uterus. The woman is given progesterone so that the lining of the womb is ready for implantation. The present process produces more fertilised **gametes** than are needed. The HFE Act permits up to two to be placed in the womb (and three in exceptional circumstances).
- *In vitro* **maturation or IVM**. In 2007 the HFEA permitted IVM as an alternative to IVF. It involves removing immature eggs from a woman's ovaries and maturing them in laboratories before fertilising them with a man's sperm. As this does not require using hormone drugs to stimulate the release of mature eggs it is therefore safer and much less expensive than IVF. It is suitable for women of less than 38 years of age who have polycystic ovaries on ultrasound scan.
- **Artificial insemination by husband or AIH**. The husband's sperm is either mechanically placed directly in the womb or fertilised using the IVF method.
- **Donors**. Instead of using husband and wife sperm and egg, a donor may be used for either or both: **donor insemination** or sperm donation (DI), **ovum donation** or egg donation (OD) and **embryo donation (ED)**. Sperm donation helps where a man's sperm are defective or may suffer from a hereditary genetic disease. The HFE Act limits the number of children to ten per donor. The social father is considered to be the legal father unless he fails to consent. Since 1996 no fee is paid to any donor.
- **Frozen eggs/sperm**. The Act was amended in 1996 to allow freezing of eggs/sperm for up to ten years. This allows for men and women undergoing dangerous operations to extract their sperm/eggs to be fertilised at a future time.

Key word

A **gamete** is a sex cell (i.e. egg or sperm) containing half the number of chromosomes (i.e. 23 for humans) and capable of fusing with a gamete of the opposite sex to produce a fertilised egg.

● **Right to know donor**. The Human Fertilisation and Embryology Authority (Disclosure of Donor Information) Regulations 2004 permit children who are aged 18 and over the right to know the identity of their donor parent as held on the HFEA's register of donors. The new regulation does not permit children to know the identity of their donor retrospectively, that is, before April 2005.

b) Rights and consent

Key question

Is the use of donor for sperm and egg going to cause identity problems for the child and parents?

As well as the general issue of whether a person has a right to a child, IVF raises more complex issues about the rights of donors. If there is a right to reproduce, then this has to be balanced against the right to be born in the best possible circumstances.

i) Right to use partner's gamete

The right to use a partner's gamete **without consent**. In the case of **Diane Blood** (1998) the HFEA had originally refused her permission to use her dead husband's sperm because he had not given written consent. Mrs Blood had taken and frozen her husband's sperm whilst he lay in a coma after he contracted bacterial meningitis in 1995. The question is whether marriage constitutes *implicit* consent given that one of the purposes of marriage is for the procreation of children. The Court of Appeal judged that in this case, though consent was not explicitly given, it could not stop her using artificial insemination outside the UK. However, is it reasonable for a child to be born knowing that his father had not intended his birth?

ii) Right to use aborted foetus' eggs

If as in the case of Diane Blood explicit consent is not always necessary then is there anything morally objectionable about using an aborted foetus' eggs? If eggs are in short supply and a female foetus has 400,000 to two million immature eggs in her ovaries, might it not be argued that rather than waste this resource it should be used to help many others? It might be argued that it could harm the child to know that its genetic parent never fully existed or was deliberately destroyed. On the other hand an objection of this kind might be more to do with taste (i.e. just a feeling of dislike) than sound reasoning. If this process became more common the child might simply be grateful to be alive whatever their origins. However, this view is inconsistent with the 'right to know' which is considered next.

Key question

Should a sperm or egg donor have a right to anonymity?

iii) Right to know a donor

When the HFE Act first became law in 1990 donors had a right to remain anonymous if they wished. This was on the recommendation

Key quote

Anonymity would give legal protection to the donor but it would also have the effect of minimising the invasion of the third party into the family.

WARNOCK, *A QUESTION OF LIFE*, PAGE 25

Key question

Should there be any age limit for a woman who wishes to use IVF?

Cross-reference

For the status of the foetus discussion see pages 37–38 above.

of **The Warnock Report** (1984) which argued that as the donor does not intend to become a father or mother, but the means for others to become parents, then they should have their identity protected by law. But the change in the 2004 law reflects a shift to the welfare of the child and the right to know more about their origins and the identity of the donor (e.g. physical characteristics, religion, occupation, interests, why he became a donor, age, surname, etc.).

iv) Right to a child in old age

A number of recent cases have questioned the usual practice of restricting IVF to younger women. For example the Romanian academic and single woman **Adriana Iliescu** (2005) gave birth to her first child at the age of 66. At the time this made her the oldest woman to give birth. Liberal commentators argued that as a woman she had a right to be a mother at any age, but fewer considered whether her child had a right to expect (all things being equal) an upbringing that could normally be provided by younger parents.

v) Right of ownership of frozen embryos

Many couples who undergo IVF preserve some embryos in a state called **cryopreservation**. But who has rights of ownership? In the important **Davis v. Davis** (1989) case in the USA the couple who had frozen some embryos subsequently divorced. In the first instance the courts gave custody to the mother as they judged it was in the embryos' best interest to be with their mother, even though the ex-husband objected. But on appeal the court ruled for joint custody on the grounds of 'procreational autonomy' of both partners. The decision was based on the view that if one of the partners does not want to be a parent this outweighs the other's interests. In 1993 the husband's wishes were respected and the embryos were destroyed. Ownership disputes often also take into account the status of the foetus and whether, for example, if the mother dies, the frozen embryos are then legally 'orphans'.

c) Normative ethical responses to IVF

i) Utilitarianism

The basic aims of IVF are the same as those of surrogacy, namely that an infertile couple can have their own child (see pages 60–61 above). For most utilitarians the use of IVF and donors depends almost entirely on the **empirical evidence**. For **act utilitarians** the key issues are whether the happiness of having a child is greater than the possible pain or risks. If there are objections to the means (the technological processes) these must be based on rational and observable facts that they do indeed cause physical or psychological harm. An objection is not a valid one if it simply appears 'unnatural' or 'odd'.

Utilitarian benefits:

- IVF helps where a woman's fallopian tubes are blocked or damaged, or when she produces anti-bodies which react to her partner's semen and kill his sperm.
- IVF allows for genetic screening for disorders and the possibility for 'engineering' where defects are found.
- DI, OD and ED enable infertile couples to have children and for the woman to go through the process of pregnancy. Unlike surrogacy there is none of the confusion in law of who the baby belongs to.
- ED has the advantage of not producing extra fertilised eggs.
- Donors could be a family member and therefore feel less alien than an anonymous donor.
- IVM is less expensive than IVF and less emotionally and physically painful.

Utilitarian risks/harm:

- IVF is often very painful from the side effects of drugs to produce eggs for 'harvesting' which often requires surgical operation for extraction.
- IVF is psychologically draining; the woman feels that her body is not her own because it is subject to many tests.
- IVF is very expensive. For example the Oxford Fertility Unit quoted in 2007 £2715 per treatment cycle excluding £600–£1200 for drugs, registration fees and charges for donor sperm or egg.
- IVF has a high chance of failure. Statistics depend on many factors but typically the percentage of live births from IVF for women less than 35 years old is about 40 per cent, dropping to 6 per cent for women over 40 years old.
- High IVF success rates can be achieved by placing several fertilised eggs back in the womb, but this increases the chance of multiple births with all the financial and emotional problems associated with having many children.
- IVF necessarily produces extra fertilised eggs which may have to be destroyed.
- Using ED a child will have two genetic parents and two social parents. This could cause identity problems with the child and a sense that the child is not fully their own with the parents.
- OD suffers from the problem that the demand for donors far outstrips supply. Should eggs be used from aborted foetuses?

The problem of how to treat discarded unwanted embryos depends at what stage the utilitarian considers the foetus is sentient or feels pain. **Preference utilitarians** such as Peter Singer (see page 29 above) find the arguments for the protection of the embryo on the grounds that it is a potential person incoherent. He argues that logically this would mean that all eggs and sperm would have to be saved if possible, and clearly this is absurd. If so then there is no rational reason why disposing of an unwanted embryo should be problematic.

> If the potential of the embryo is so crucial, why do all sides agree they would not object to disposing of the egg and sperm before they have been combined? An egg and a drop of seminal fluid, viewed collectively, also have the potential to develop into a mature human being.
>
> (Peter Singer, *Technology and Procreation: How Far Should We Go?*, Technology Review 88 number 2, 1985, page 27)

ii) Natural law

Key question

If parents may form a family through adoption, by analogy should this also permit the use of IVF?

The natural law position is most clearly stated by the **Roman Catholic Church**, although there are others who share some of its non-religious reasoning. The Catholic view is most clearly expressed in the Pope's instruction *Donum Vitae* (1987) or 'the gift of life'. The natural law position is based on **two major premises**:

- Life begins at conception and although not yet fully actualised as a human person it has all the potentials to do so. The human embryo, therefore, must be respected from the moment of conception onward.
- The intention of the physical act of intercourse is to procreate; anything which separates the unitive from the procreative has therefore altered the intention of the sexual act. Artificial forms of reproduction effectively treat the child as a commodity.

However, *Donum Vitae* does not reject all forms of reproductive technologies. The Church only objects to those techniques which bypass normal intercourse. It therefore recommends **naprotechnology** which analyses why a woman is unable to conceive and offers surgical or drug-based solutions.

Key words

Naprotechnology or **natural procreative technology** is a women's health science that monitors and maintains a woman's reproductive and gynaecological health. It provides medical and surgical treatments which work naturally with her reproductive system.

Licit (lawful) and **illicit** (unlawful) are important terms in natural law.

Donum Vitae rejects all forms of reproductive technologies which bypass the act of intercourse for the following reasons:

- The primary objection to **IVF** is that the process means creating more embryos than can be transferred to the woman. This means either passing on the embryo to another couple or destroying them. Both options negate the first major premise stated above; although passing on the embryo is the lesser of two evils it still has the effect of treating the embryo as a thing not a person.
- All **experimentation** on early embryos (up to 14 days) is **illicit**. Freezing of embryos is also condemned as it can cause damage (even death) to the embryo and fails to give the embryo its natural place to develop in the 'maternal shelter'.
- The use of a **donor** is illicit as it introduces a 'third party' into the marriage. Not only is this **adultery** but it confuses the natural *order* in which parents and children understand their relationship

to each other. This is especially acute if the donor is a family member. It can be confusing for a child to find out that the person he calls his aunt is in fact his biological mother and that his mother is his biological aunt. It is part of natural law that a child can expect the love and security which is part of being biologically related to both parents.

- **AIH** might appear to be an extension of the natural process and does not introduce a third party into the relationship, as a donor gamete would do. But *symbolically* it destroys the wholeness of the spiritual–physical relationship between husband and wife.

Some have suggested that IVF should be compared to **adoption**. Adopting a child who is not biologically one's own doesn't devalue the child and a childless couple can form a loving family with the adopted child.

But this view is rejected because the **intention** does not fulfil the second major premise (see above). Adoption occurs when a child has been abandoned by its natural parents, for whatever reasons; the intention here is to provide a home for an already existing child. The only exception could be in extreme cases where a couple offer to 'adopt' an embryo which would otherwise be destroyed.

iii) Virtue ethics

The virtue ethicist might look at the intentions of a couple seeking to use reproductive technology, but an important area which so far has not been considered is the professional and ethical conduct of the doctor, physician or surgeon. In Chapter 1 (see page 5 above) we considered two versions of virtue ethics: the pure virtue-orientated approach and the principle-orientated approach. The latter approach is the one which neatly balances the important principles of the medical profession and its corresponding virtues.

The virtue ethicist argues that the intrusive and complex nature of IVF requires more than merely offering a service. As we saw earlier (page 5) William May argued that when a doctor makes a promise it is a performative act; it creates a new situation in which the patient knows his life is valued and cared for.

Consider how a virtue ethicist complements Beauchamp and Childress' suggested four professional medical principles with regard to IVF:

- **Autonomy** (freedom to exercise one's will) might correspond with the virtue of **honesty** to outline all the risks involved. Feminist commentators have praised the openness of many hospitals and clinics who have published realistic figures of success and failure. Honesty therefore enhances the ability of the surgeon to act with greater freedom and that of the couple to know that it is their welfare the surgeon has at the heart of his treatment.

- **Non-maleficence** (avoiding harm) might correspond with the virtues of **perseverance** and **humility** to admit to lack of knowledge and not to offer risky procedures. It might be tempting for a doctor to presume superior knowledge where it might be lacking or to carry out a new procedure because it presents a new challenge. Humility reminds him that his role as physician is not to cause harm but to consider his patient first.
- **Beneficence** (producing benefits) might correspond with the virtues of **benevolence** and **compassion**. Hospitals and clinics are as much subject to the market place as any other business. Some have likened IVF to the 'new oil' and there are sufficiently desperate couples who will spend life savings on fertility treatment to sway a hospital to offer treatment which may not be entirely necessary. As Alasdair MacIntyre has argued, our society today is more often governed by bureaucracy than goodness.
- **Justice** (distributing benefits, risks and costs fairly) might correspond with the **distribution** of the doctor's services and skills equitably. Some have argued that this cannot be a doctor's individual decision because he works according to the rules of the hospital. But the virtue ethicist here is referring to the quality of time and care he gives to each patient. He might of course feel that society should fund IVF so that infertile couples from poor backgrounds should have equal access to treatment. This depends on whether society or the medical profession regard infertility as an illness or an unfortunate condition.

iv) Revealed ethics

Strong sanctity of life Christian teaching may or may not share the natural law ethics expressed by the Roman Catholic Church (see natural law above). We have already seen the ambiguity and dangers of surrogacy (see pages 72–73 above) as expressed in the story of Abraham and Sarah.

However, for conservative Christians who do not base their arguments so much on natural law but on the Bible, IVF can be seen to support the family as an important aspect of Christian life. AIH in particular poses no immediate ethical objections as it merely makes possible what was intended in the act of sexual intercourse. There are no third parties (donors or surrogates) and the commandment not to commit adultery (Exodus 20:14) is respected.

Weak sanctity of life Christian teaching argues that respect for human life does not need to be predicated on an absolute genetic or biological relationship to the child to be valid. For example in the Church of England's revised report *Personal Origins* (1996) it argues that IVF and the use of donors may be based legitimately on the **analogy of adoption**. But it argues that for this to make theological and psychological sense there must be *openness* and honesty from the start. Providing a child knows how and why they have been brought into being then the question of exact genetic origin becomes less important. In other words if a child can understand the *story* of their own identity in terms of a willed and loving action, this is the essential ingredient for their own sense of self-worth.

The report is aware that being open and honest is not without its problems.

- In order for the child to feel secure, grandparents, friends and existing children, not just parents, have to accept that the child is needed and loved.
- By the same token a great deal of psychological damage can be done when a child is told that he or she was a 'mistake' and that conception was unintentional.
- Just as in adoption, children often *do* want to know about their origins.
- The analogy with adoption is not entirely similar. Whereas in the case of adoption there is a birth mother with her own history and reasons for giving away a child, a donor did not create or give away a life. Even so it might be argued that the insistence that egg or sperm should not be sold but given freely as an act of generosity acknowledges that the provision of genetic material is more than inert substance. This acknowledges that there are implications for the future welfare of the child to consider for which the donor may feel, in some way, responsible.
- It is understandable therefore why some children should want to know why they are the way they are, and in order for their own story to be complete they need more than a genetic or biological account of their donor.
- This might lead to complicated emotional problems: an intrusion of the donor's child later into his life, where he or she may have their own family, may not be welcome; the donor may not wish to make contact with the child.

Situationist or liberal Christian arguments resist the anti-rational phobias of conservative Christians to technology. Joseph Fletcher, for example, provocatively regarded artificial insemination as being more human than natural reproduction, because human reason is able to control nature through technology. In fact artificial insemination offers a more responsible and loving means of creating a family as the screening processes enable the gametes of the parents to be checked against abnormalities.

Key quote

Man is a maker and a selector and a designer, and the more rationally contrived and deliberate anything is, the more human it is. Any attempt to set up an antinomy between natural and biological reproduction, on the one hand, and artificial or designed reproduction, on the other, is absurd.

JOSEPH FLETCHER, *HUMANHOOD: ESSAYS IN BIOMEDICAL ETHICS*, PAGES 87–88

Summary diagram

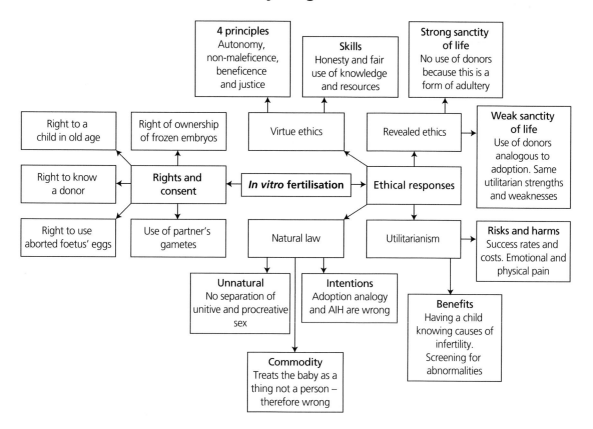

Study guide

By the end of this chapter, you should have considered whether a person or a couple have a right to a child or whether a child is a gift. This view will depend on what is meant by a right and whether the idea of a gift is meant in a religious or non-religious sense. For those who are unable to have children naturally the question of surrogacy has been considered. You will have assessed whether this form of assisted reproduction is ethically acceptable by considering the viewpoints of various normative ethical systems. In addition you will have also weighed up the use of IVF and the issues this raises (such as the use of donors and what to do with unwanted fertilised eggs).

Revision checklist

Can you define the following words...?

- surrogacy; commissioning parents; genetic parents; surrogate mother; partial and full surrogacy; commercial and altruistic surrogacy
- IVF, IVM, AIH, ED.

Do you know:

- Article 16 (UN Declaration) on the right to form a family
- the biblical story of Abraham and Hagar and the problem of slavery
- the law on surrogacy
- the natural law view of the unitive/procreative purpose of sex.

Can you explain the views of the following ethical approaches to the issue of IVF:

- revealed or religious ethics
- natural ethics
- virtue ethics
- utilitarian ethics.

Can you give arguments for and against:

- the view that surrogacy harms the long-term welfare of the child
- the view that surrogacy contradicts the notion of motherhood
- using sperm/egg donors in IVF.

Essay question

1a. *Explain the arguments which support a woman's right to a child.*

1b. *'A child is a gift not a right.' Discuss.*

The essay could begin with a brief definition of a right as a universal entitlement either in terms of natural rights or human rights. This then needs linking to a woman's right to a child. A natural rights argument might suggest that as a woman's body is uniquely designed to have children then she has a right to have a child unhindered. Human rights could be supported by the socio-economic or welfare rights position that the well-being of the woman and society are contingent on having children. The essay should point out the ambiguities of whether a woman has a right to infertility treatment if she is unable to have a child.

The evaluative essay (1b) might begin with the view supported by natural law and revealed ethics that as sex between husband and wife is both procreative and unitive the product of a child is a blessing on that relationship but not a right. However, this does not take into account that infertility may be seen as an illness and a couple may have a right to treatment which might involve IVF or even surrogacy. Reproductive technologies can cause complex problems of identity and the analysis will have to consider whether an overwhelming desire for a child might make it a commodity.

Further essay questions

2a   Explain the aims of virtue ethics.
2b   Assess the view that virtue ethics offers the best approach to issues of infertility.

3   'All types of surrogacy are wrong because they treat the baby as a thing not a person.' Discuss.

4   To what extent do revealed ethics consider that the use of IVF for infertile couples is good?

6

EMBRYO RESEARCH

Chapter checklist

This chapter considers whether it is right to use and destroy embryos in order to advance scientific knowledge about the causes of infertility, detection of abnormalities in embryos and improvement to contraception. This raises issues about the status of the embryo and whether or not it is a person or potential person. Various normative ethical responses to embryo research are surveyed.

Case study
Designer baby fears over heart gene test approval

Embryo research is one example of medical research, and it is an emotive subject. Take for example this headline from *The Times*: 'Designer baby fears over heart gene test approval' (15 December 2007). The headline suggests that medical science is doing things which we the public should be very worried about. Secondly, that genetic alteration of foetuses is unnecessary and superfluous and we should be very suspicious of those who are using it. Finally, by using the term 'baby' there is an assumption that the alteration of genes is being done to human persons without their consent and if true this would be a violation of basic human rights.

This particular case illustrates the problems encountered by current medical research.

- The Human Fertilisation and Embryology Association gave permission to screen foetuses thought to possess the gene familial hypercholesterolaemia (FH) which usually predisposes adults to have high cholesterol levels in the blood, one of the main causes of coronary heart disease.
- About 1 in 500 British people carries the FH gene. If two people **heterozygous** for the FH gene have children, there is a 1 in 4 chance of each child having the disease. The disease can therefore affect one in 250,000 people.

Key word

Heterozygous means, in this case, that the adult has both the disease-causing recessive gene and the normal dominant gene. They do not show symptoms of the disease but have the potential, as a carrier, to pass on the gene to their offspring.

- The condition can be treated with drugs but it does not always work well and the risk cannot be removed entirely.
- It cannot be detected in adults very easily until a person suffers a heart attack.
- Genetic screening will allow a single cell to be taken from an IVF embryo at the eight cell stage and tested for the defective gene. If it has the heterozygous FH gene the embryo will be discarded and the test can be carried out on the other embryos. If the others are free from the genes then the parents will have to decide whether to implant all remaining healthy embryos or discard or freeze the others.

Paul Serhal, who had been given the licence to carry out the screening, gave the following summary of the moral issues:

This obnoxious disease can cause cardiovascular accidents from a very young age. Ideally, we will find embryos with no FH genes, but it is possible that we will not and it will be up to the patients to choose. Some people would think twice about using embryos that they know have a risky gene, and others would say you shouldn't screen out a condition that can be managed so people can live with it. It will be an awkward choice.

This case therefore illustrates a number of interrelated issues which are the subject matter of this chapter.

1 The reasons for embryo research

In order for medical science to progress at some stage in research experimentation has to take place on humans and not through computer modelling or animal experimentation. In many cases adult humans, even the scientists themselves, have volunteered to try out a new drug or treatment. But some areas of research require experimentation to be carried out on the foetus. For example embryo experimentation is used for:

- **Contraception**. There is a need for alternative means to the contraceptive pill used by many women because the pill can cause undesirable side effects. Research is being carried out for a vaccine which will cause the sperm to be rejected by the ova using the woman's antibodies. A vaccine has worked in animals but it now needs to be tested on humans. This can be done using IVF in the first instance. But there is always a possibility that an embryo might be created using this method.

Cross-reference

See page 90 to see what the zona pellucida is.

- **Infertility**. IVF also provides the opportunity for a better understanding of infertility. The majority of infertility cases are caused by male defective sperm where sperm cannot penetrate the *zona pellucida* (of the ovum). Tests carried out PCT (post coital test) on human ova and embryo can provide invaluable data which can help in the understanding of the causes of male infertility. Experimentation can also discover why so many embryos die on being placed in the womb.
- **Detection of genetic abnormalities**. It has been found that 30 per cent of pre-embryos formed by IVF are chromosomally abnormal. This may not necessarily be caused by IVF, it is just that the process allows us to know more because it is impossible to know the status of an 8-cell embryo *in vivo* (in the womb). However, embryo biopsy allows the cells to be investigated at the 4–8 cell stage. This can help reveal abnormalities. The use of embryos is therefore needed to perfect this testing stage.

2 The law and embryo research

Key word

Pre-embryo describes the embryo from conception to 14 days old.

The **Human Fertilisation and Embryology Act** (1990) permits research to be carried out on the human embryo up to the fourteenth day of gestation – that is, up to the point where the **primitive streak** appears. The Act refers, perhaps controversially, to the embryo up to this stage as the **pre-embryo**. The term pre-embryo has become widely used, but as it implies that the embryo is not a human being, many find it offensive and prefer the term 'early embryo'.

a) The Warnock Report

The Act was originally based on the recommendations of **The Warnock Report** (1984). The Warnock Report's justification for embryo research is essentially a utilitarian one. If experiments on the pre-embryo can further scientific knowledge to help overcome problems of infertility and other genetic problems in the future, then the goods outweigh any other emotional or moral hesitations. The revolutionary position which The Warnock Report established was that a 14-day-old 'pre-embryo' is not a person but should nevertheless have some protection under law, but not the same protection as the embryo *in vivo* (in the womb).

Pre-embryos can be obtained in two ways. Firstly, they might be produced as spare embryos through IVF infertility treatment (with the intention of being transferred to the mother) and, secondly, they might be produced deliberately and specifically for research purposes.

b) The Human Fertilisation and Embryology Act

The law states that experimentation of embryos *in vitro* (outside the womb) is to be regulated under licence by the HFE authority. No experimentation is permitted on the pre-embryo beyond 14 days (excluding any time in which the embryo has been frozen) and the embryo may not be placed in the womb of a woman (or non-human animal).

The Human Fertilisation and Embryology Act presently states in paragraph 3 the following regulations:

Prohibitions in connection with embryos

1 No person shall:
   a bring about the creation of an embryo, or
   b keep or use an embryo, except in pursuance of a licence.

2 No person shall place in a woman:
   a a live embryo other than a human embryo, or
   b any live gametes other than human gametes.

3 A licence cannot authorise:
   a keeping or using an embryo after the appearance of the primitive streak,
   b placing an embryo in any animal,
   c keeping or using an embryo in any circumstances in which regulations prohibit its keeping or use, or
   d replacing a nucleus of a cell of an embryo with a nucleus taken from a cell of any person, embryo or subsequent development of an embryo.*

4 For the purposes of subsection (3)(a) above, the primitive streak is to be taken to have appeared in an embryo not later than the end of the period of 14 days beginning with the day when the gametes are mixed, not counting any time during which the embryo is stored.

(*Human Fertilisation and Embryology Act*, 1990)

* The Human Reproductive Cloning Act (2001) states that 'A person who places in a woman a human embryo which has been created otherwise than by fertilisation is guilty of an offence', thereby making it illegal to use reproductive cloning.

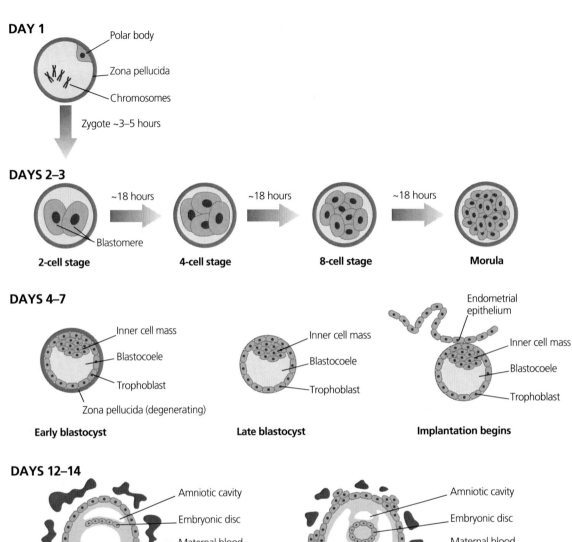

DAY 1

Polar body

Zona pellucida

Chromosomes

Zygote ~3–5 hours

DAYS 2–3

~18 hours   ~18 hours   ~18 hours

Blastomere

2-cell stage   **4-cell stage**   **8-cell stage**   **Morula**

DAYS 4–7

Inner cell mass

Blastocoele

Trophoblast

Zona pellucida (degenerating)

Inner cell mass

Blastocoele

Trophoblast

Endometrial epithelium

Inner cell mass

Blastocoele

Trophoblast

Early blastocyst   **Late blastocyst**   **Implantation begins**

DAYS 12–14

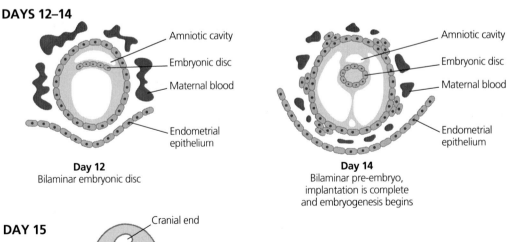

Amniotic cavity

Embryonic disc

Maternal blood

Endometrial epithelium

Amniotic cavity

Embryonic disc

Maternal blood

Endometrial epithelium

Day 12
Bilaminar embryonic disc

Day 14
Bilaminar pre-embryo,
implantation is complete
and embryogenesis begins

DAY 15

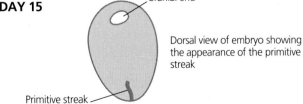

Cranial end

Dorsal view of embryo showing
the appearance of the primitive
streak

Primitive streak

Preimplantation of embryo development.

3 Normative ethical responses to embryo research

A key consideration of embryo research and the use of embryonic stem cells (see below) is the status of the early embryo/pre-embryo. Chapter 2 looked at some of the factors which determine the moral status of the embryo and from this two broad positions emerged: the **vitalist** position, which claims that humans have an 'enduring self', and the sentience position, which suggests that human personhood develops according to the degree of **sentience** (the ability to feel pain or have desires) or consciousness.

a) Strong sanctity of life

Vitalists find it morally reprehensible that human life of any kind should be subject to experimentation. The vitalist position holds that from the moment of conception the cells are irreversibly a human being and even if it is not yet an actual person it has the potential to become so. Revealed law supports this position that humans are created in the image of God (Genesis 1:27) and 'knitted together' and given life in the womb by God (Psalm 139:13–16). This is sufficient reason for the embryo to be protected and to reject the notion that even good ends can justify the means by inflicting harm on the foetus. The argument might be expressed as:

- Every innocent human being has a right to life (major premise).
- A human embryo is (or has the potential to be) an innocent human being (minor premise).
- Therefore the human embryo has a right to life (conclusion).

Strong sanctity of life arguments reject any weakening of the rule on the grounds that it is the beginning of a **slippery slope**. Once society accepts that experiments may be done on non-consenting people, then as seen in the Nazi regimes atrocities may be performed in the name of medical research.

b) Preference utilitarianism

Key question

Is there a difference between taking an interest and having an interest in one's future?

The sentience position rejects the strong sanctity of the life vitalist argument for two reasons.

Firstly, even if the embryo is a human being it is not a single human *person* because until the development of the **primitive streak** the embryo (see picture on page 20) could become one or more individual beings. Peter Singer's position is widely accepted by many utilitarians who reject vitalism. He argues that even vitalists have to base their arguments on a potential life position; it then follows that sperm, egg and pre-embryo all have the potential to become several persons or no persons at all. If this is so then it is incoherent to say that life at this stage is in any way unique. It is only after 14 days when the cells have developed into one or more individuals that we can distinguish it from a pre-embryo and only now can we give it moral consideration.

Secondly, Singer argues that for the vitalists' major premise to be true we have to give human beings some special mental qualities which set them apart from other animals – such as the ability to look forward to tomorrow, the ability to form sophisticated relationships and the ability to determine one's future. Now if this is true then many human beings would not pass the test; most children would not, for example, be persons on these grounds. And if this is so then pre-embryos would certainly not be considered persons. For the argument to work at all, Singer suggests that the bar has to be set much lower by using sentience (the ability to feel pain and pleasure) as the defining quality. But even with this much broader definition the pre-embryo is not included. So, Singer's argument can be summarised in this way:

Key quote

We believe the minimal characteristic needed to give the embryo a claim to consideration is sentience, or the capacity to feel pleasure or pain. Until that point is reached, the embryo does not have any interests and, like other non-sentient beings (a human egg, for example), cannot be harmed – in a morally relevant sense – by anything we do.

PETER SINGER (ED.), *EMBRYO EXPERIMENTATION*, PAGE 73

- Every sentient human being has a right to life and respect of interests.
- The pre-embryo is not a sentient human being.
- Therefore the pre-embryo has no right to life and no loss of interests.

c) Natural law

Natural law vitalists reject Singer's pre-embryo lack of interests argument. They feel that he has confused '*having* interest in' with '*taking* interest in'. It is true that an early embryo (note *not* a pre-embryo) does not have the mental/physical facilities to *take* interest in anything, but it does *have* a general interest that its life should be preserved and nurtured. Helen Watt explains:

> For example, infants are seen as having interests in their future ration-al awareness. Even if a child who undergoes a certain harm – for example, mental damage due to neglect – will never come to regret that harm, it is seen as against the child's interests to let the harm occur. The view that a child can have interests only in the things which he or she can now desire, or will desire in the future, is not borne out by either common sense, or by standard medical practice.
>
> (Helen Watt, *Life and Death in Healthcare Ethics*, page 10)

This view is reinforced by standard Roman Catholic teaching that 'From the first moment of his existence a human being must be recognised as having the rights of a person – among which is the inviolable right of every innocent being to life' (*Catechism of the Catholic Church*, page 489).

d) Weak sanctity of life

Cross-reference

See page 26 above for principles of the weak sanctity of life position.

Finally, there are those who hold a **weak vitalist** position which agrees with many aspects of Singer's argument. Those who hold some kind of '**delayed ensoulment**' view meet Singer's challenge that it is only post–14 days that a life can truly be considered an individual life. For the Christian weak sanctity of life supporter, being 'alive' is not sufficient unless a person can express himself physically *and* spiritually. Furthermore, it might be argued that it is the most loving thing to do to act for the flourishing of other future lives. Foetal experimentation is one crucial way of doing this. But the problem for the weak vitalist is what criterion determines when it can be considered a life – it could be Locke's consciousness criterion or Singer's less stringent sentience criterion. As the authors of the Church of England's *Personal Origins* (1996) state, there is no consensus amongst Christians as to the ontological status of the early embryo. Joseph Fletcher represents the most liberal view:

> *The metaphysical or religious belief that fetuses are persons is a perfectly legitimate act of faith, but there is no way to prove it or show it… Most of us, when we look at the consequences of that belief, reject it because consistently acting on it would lower the quality of life in our children and paralyze our standards of reproductive medicine. To treat live fetuses as untouchable is absurd.*
>
> (Joseph Fletcher, *Humanhood: Essays in Biomedical Ethics*, page 96)

The weak sanctity of life argument rejects the assumption that by weakening the absolute nature of the sanctity of life this logically necessitates a **slippery slope**. The fact that we *can* do something doesn't *necessarily* mean that we will do it. In Fletcher's situational ethics his 'pragmatic principle' of love or prudence ensures that we always act in the best interests of society. However, this means that there is still a need for guidelines (he is not antinomian) which will guard against experimentation for its own sake. But strong rules which forbid all medical research on foetuses are contrary to the basic principle of respect for human welfare.

Summary diagram

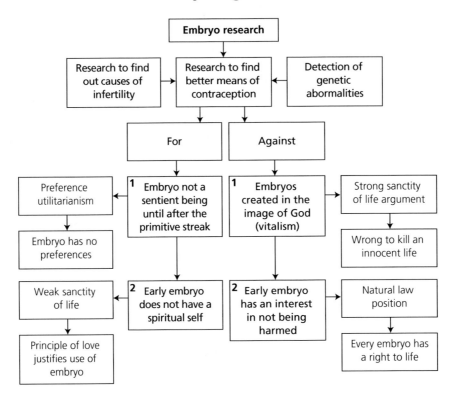

Study guide

By the end of the chapter, you should have considered the reasons why embryo research has been carried out to improve scientific understanding of pre-embryo development, to assist with our understanding of infertility, the improvement of contraception and detection of foetal abnormalities. The main ethical consideration focuses on the status of the pre-embryo. You should be able to compare and contrast the vitalist and sentient positions held by advocates of the sanctity of life and utilitarianism respectively.

Revision checklist

Can you explain:

■ the vitalist arguments for when human embryos become persons
■ the distinction between the early embryo *having* interests in and *taking* interests in
■ why The Warnock Report established a radical position on embryo research.

Do you know:

■ two reasons why embryos are needed for research
■ the present law on embryo research
■ what is meant by the primitive streak.

Can you give the arguments for and against:

■ Peter Singer's preference utilitarian argument for the use of pre-embryos for research
■ the coherency of the weak sanctity of life.

Essay question

1. Assess the view that ethical objections which forbid research on pre-embryos to improve the human quality of life are irrational.

This is a question that requires both knowledge and understanding as well as evaluation skills. The ethical objections rest on the major premise that as the pre-foetus is an actual or potential person then according to natural (and revealed) law it should receive the absolute protection due to all innocent persons. This view will need to be explained carefully and contrasted with the preference utilitarian view (of Peter Singer) that as the pre-embryo has the potential to become more than one person it has no preferences or loss of interests.

The evaluative element could focus on what makes the vitalist position irrational. It might be considered irrational because the notion of a potential person cannot be demonstrated and relies on an a priori belief which is itself irrational (i.e. that life is God-given). However, the counter-argument might consider that the embryo may not 'take an interest' in its fate but would certainly 'have an interest' in survival. A possible conclusion might be that if there is strong scientific evidence to support improvement to the quality of human life this should outweigh any other objections.

Further essay questions

2a   Explain the purpose of human embryo research.
2b   Assess the view that a preference utilitarian approach to human embryo research is the best one.

3a   Explain the aims of the sanctity of life arguments.
3b   'Sanctity of life arguments should not permit embryo research.' Discuss.

4   'Embryo research is an offence against human dignity.' Discuss.

7

GENE THERAPY AND
THE USE OF STEM CELLS

Chapter checklist

This chapter looks at testing of human genes for abnormalities and considers the use of embryonic and adult stem cells to treat severe degenerative diseases such as Alzheimer's. The controversial argument for using gene therapy to improve or enhance the quality of life is discussed as well as the debate about compulsory genetic screening and the problem of confidentiality. Various normative ethical responses are surveyed.

Case study
The Senate vote and presidential veto, July 2006

On July 18, 2006, the US Senate voted to expand federal funding of embryonic stem cell research, passing a bill that had passed the House the year before. The next day President Bush, as he had promised to do, vetoed the bill, the first of his administration. President Bush, at a news conference at the White House explaining his veto, said the bill would be 'crossing a moral line and would support the taking of innocent human life.' He was surrounded by dozens of Snowflake children, born from embryo-adoption programs, and by their parents. 'These boys and girls are not spare parts,' the President affirmed.

Representative Nancy Pelosi of California, the House minority leader, retorted that Bush's veto was 'saying "no" to hope.' And Senator Orrin Hatch agreed, saying the veto 'sets back embryonic stem cell research another year or so.'

(Gregory Pence, *Classic Cases in Medical Ethics* (fifth edition), page 130)

President Bush's reaction to the use of embryo stem cell research highlights the tension between wanting to provide cures for various diseases but at the same time wishing to respect human life. But is the use of embryonic stem cells necessarily crossing a moral line? How are these lines to be decided? What treatment justifies the use of stem cells?

1 Types of therapy

The first consideration is to establish the status of genetic defect. Defects might be described in two ways. Firstly, a defect is something which is traditionally regarded as a disease which will cause the person to die early or suffer greatly. Secondly, a defect might be considered as something which frustrates a person's future development. The therapy of each kind of defect can be described as follows:

- **Negative therapy**: that is, the removal of defects or diseases by selection.
- **Positive therapy**: that is, the enhancement or improvement of human qualities by alteration of certain genes.

There are two ways in which genes might be engineered:

- **Passive control**. Couples can be tested prior to having a child for genetic counselling or encouraging them *not* to have a child, or during pregnancy to have an abortion or to select only healthy embryos using IVF.
- **Active control**. Direct interference either in the form of **somatic gene cell therapy** whereby the alteration or addition of genes to cells in the body change its characteristics (but not for future generations) or **germ line gene cell therapy**. This latter process constitutes the alteration or addition of gametes (that is, the genes in the sperm or egg) of an adult or embryo which will cause all future generations to be modified as well.

However, at present active gene therapy is still in its early days. The most desirable outcome for active negative therapy would be to replace the abnormal gene with a normal one at exactly the same site as the chromosome. Some scientists hope that in the future they will be able to deliver an artificial human chromosome with a normal gene already on it without disrupting existing DNA.

2 Risks and benefits

The consequential risks of somatic gene therapy are caused by the methods used to deliver the gene to a cell. A healthy gene is introduced into the virus' genome which is then injected into the body. The virus infects the cells in the body and with luck transfers the healthy gene into the body.

Other methods include injecting the DNA directly into the cells inside the body or first extracting DNA and then fusing it with the healthy gene and then injecting it back. Clearly the possible benefits are huge. It means that diseases which are usually fatal or severely debilitating can now be treated, even though this does not mean a long-term cure.

However, somatic therapy is not an exact science and it can cause disorders (such as leukaemia in children) as well as offer temporary treatment. The risk with germ line therapy is that it could slightly alter the gene pool for future generations (see below for the moral arguments).

3 Genetic enhancement

Key question

Should medicine only be used to eliminate or relieve diseases?

How does one decide where one condition is a defect and the other an improvement unless there is an already established view of the 'normal' human being? Which of the following would be considered the removal of a defect or an improvement?

- the correction of the genetic causes of cystic fibrosis
- the correction of the chromosomal abnormality which causes Down's syndrome
- the manipulation of the sex chromosomes that determine the sex of a child
- the manipulation of the gene or genes (if they exist) which cause homosexuality
- the manipulation of the genes which determine a person's height
- the manipulation of the genes which determine a person's skin colour.

The general reaction is that it is wrong to create 'designer babies' (positive therapy) but self-evident that defects should be removed or treated (negative therapy). The rejection of 'improvement' or 'enhancement' rests on two assumptions. Firstly, the anti-reductionist claim which considers that no single gene can ever adequately determine a major aspect of a person's character and, secondly, there is the fear that improvement might lead to the world of **eugenics** – the deliberate engineering of certain types of human beings based on an ideology of what constitutes the perfect person. Both these ideas are challenged by the film *Gattaca* (1997). In particular it illustrates the possibility that if improvement were really to become a reality then society could consciously justify discriminating against people who had not been genetically improved on the grounds that they were inferior and less reliable than those born in the new eugenically superior way.

Key word

Eugenics comes from the Greek meaning 'well born'. The term eugenics has been used to refer to the process of selective breeding with the aim of improving society.

a) The coherency of the term 'enhancement'

However, the notion of improvement or enhancement is problematic in a number of ways:

- **All therapy is enhancement.** The use of vaccines, drugs and antibiotics all help the body to return to homeostasis (the constant state of the internal environment).

- **Treatment might start as therapy and then become enhancement**. For example the use of growth hormones for a child who is very undersized might be used even for a child of average height.

The notion of enhancement depends on what the aim of the treatment is and how it is to be achieved. Thomas Murray argues that when we use the term 'enhancement' it is usually used as a 'boundary term' to refer to a problematic area which needs careful moral consideration. Enhancement can be used in a very positive sense to refer to the way in which we all work to develop our skills and potentials in order to flourish as human beings. So, parents who aim to bring up their children in the best possible way will want to give their children immunisations and injections against various diseases. In fact it might be argued that a parent who does not do these things is negligent and morally irresponsible.

But Murray doesn't think there should be free licence to allow enhancements of any kind. He sets out five responses (*The Oxford Handbook of Bioethics*, pages 498–501) to those who argue that there should be no restraint in terms of medical enhancement:

1 **Incoherency**. Some argue that there is no rational basis for distinguishing acceptable and unacceptable means because there is no clear understanding of what enhancement means (for example an athlete who uses steroids to enhance his performance is no different from an athlete who uses top of the range running shoes). But Murray argues not all means are the same to achieve a given end. For example cheating to win a game undermines the integrity of the game itself. The incoherency argument ignores complexity of ends. These may be easy to calculate in a sport but in life the ends are far more complex than this.

2 **Line drawing**. Some argue that, although there is a difference on a scale between unnecessary enhancement and legitimate enhancement (or therapy), drawing a cut-off line is arbitrary and therefore indefensible. But Murray argues that this is based on a confused understanding of the meaning of arbitrary. One definition of arbitrary means 'for no good reason' but the other definition is that there is a good reason for this choice even though there may be good reasons for other choices. The point is that *this line* can be defended. For example if we make up a game we could have any number of rules but it is sensible and possible to agree on a set of rules for this game. In other words, society can coherently set boundaries as to what it accepts as legitimate forms of enhancement.

3 **Liberty**. A powerful popular view of the liberty argument put forward by J.S. Mill is that as it is my life (or my body) I can do with it as I wish. But Murray argues that liberty only means

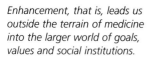

Key quote

Enhancement, that is, leads us outside the terrain of medicine into the larger world of goals, values and social institutions.

THOMAS MURRAY, *THE OXFORD HANDBOOK OF BIOETHICS*, PAGE 494

Key quote

The slogan 'He who dies with the most toys wins' is an eloquent (one hopes ironic) testimony to the folly of simplistic, shallow, quantative measures of one's life.

THOMAS MURRAY, *THE OXFORD HANDBOOK OF BIOETHICS*, PAGE 498

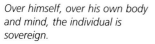

Key quote

Over himself, over his own body and mind, the individual is sovereign.

J.S. MILL, *ON LIBERTY*

something when joined to the virtues of dignity, agency and efficacy. Too much personal liberty of parents over children can be damaging just as much as a very pushy parent seeking to 'enhance' their child's life can cause great damage with overly high expectations of them.

4 **Resistance is futile**. Some argue that as society's boundaries are always changing in the quest to improve society, there is no point in resistance. For example, look at the large numbers of people who are willing to use surgery to enhance their looks. But Murray argues this is not a moral argument, merely an observation. The fact that many people do something doesn't make it right, especially when we feel that the imposition of rules (e.g. rules against theft, murder, child abuse, etc.) is necessary for their civilising effects on society.

5 **Promethean**. Some have argued that it is a special human characteristic that people are able to create their own image of themselves. This should not be stopped but encouraged; it indicates how humans are able to control their biological destiny. For example some have argued that anorexia is not bad but a means of a woman shaping her own image. Murray argues that this is an extraordinary view; anorexia is self-destructive and the argument is based on a naive understanding of the complex relationship of self and environment. Anorexia is usually the result of low esteem, not a romantic notion of heroism over nature.

Key word

Promethean means using human intelligence to further our own existence. The idea is based on the Greek myth where Prometheus stole fire from Zeus for humans to use.

Just a matter of choice: is Michael Jackson's surgery to enhance his face a legitimate use of medical resources?

b) Positive and non-medical gene therapy

Although many feel that it would be quite wrong for doctors to select a pre-embryo whose genes are predisposed to make it more athletic so that the child will grow up to become a very good football player, others argue that medicine has a wider role than merely eliminating diseases. Moreover, medicine has no eternal or intrinsic purpose and if nature provides the possibilities of enhancement then it seems reasonable to exploit them.

Julian Savulescu argues that the distinction between non-medical and medical gene therapy is a false one because of the intimate relationship between our environment and genetic/molecular make-up. For example remotivation therapy can help humans by changing brain molecular levels (neurotrophines) and IQs can be enhanced and improved through stimulating environments. There is even some experimental suggestion that these changes can be genetically passed on to the next generation. If this is true then improving a child's diet is no different from other forms of genetic intervention. Child abuse/neglect, Savulescu argues, can be just as irreversible as direct genetic changes.

Savulescu concludes his argument with an appeal to a form of virtue ethics. However, whereas many argue that risk is a vice to be avoided, he makes it an important part of being human. What matters in the end is enabling us to flourish using whatever resources we have available to live well allowing for all the risks. In fact there is a natural imperative to use our skills to enhance or improve whatever aspects of our lives make us happy. He concludes:

> *Beneficence – the moral obligation to benefit people – provides a strong reason to enhance people in so far as the biological enhancement increases their chance of having a better life. But can biological enhancements increase people's opportunities for well-being? There are reasons to believe they might.*

(Julian Savulescu, *The Oxford Handbook of Bioethics*, page 523)

4 Screening and knowledge

Screening is used to diagnose whether a person is suffering from a genetic defect. There are broadly five different ways in which genetic screening may take place.

1 **Pre-implantation**: the embryo is screened during IVF but only a few conditions can be detected at the moment (e.g. cystic fibrosis, Duchenne muscular dystrophy, Tay-Sachs disease, sickle cell disease – all single gene diseases). This method poses the question whether only healthy pre-embryos should be selected and the others discarded.

2 **In the womb**: amniocentesis is an invasive method used to test for chromosome and chemical abnormalities. This is often used for older mothers (35 years and above) where there is a higher chance of foetal abnormalities. Invasive screening can cause harm to the foetus but it poses the moral dilemma for the mother as to what she should do if the baby is severely abnormal.

Key quote

Why should we allow environmental manipulations that alter our biology but not direct biological manipulations?

JULIAN SAVULESCU, *THE OXFORD HANDBOOK OF BIOETHICS*, PAGE 522

Key word

Amniocentesis is when a small amount of amniotic fluid is taken from the womb. It contains foetal DNA which can be tested. It can cause harm to the foetus.

3 **Newborn**: it is standard practice to screen newborns for phenylketuria (PKU), which if left undetected can lead to severe mental retardation, galactosemia (body's ability to process galactose in milk) and sickle cell anaemia (which can be fatal). All these diseases can be treated (not cured) if known about early on.

4 **Carrier**: aimed at adults who have 'autosomal recessive' (AR) disorders and X-linked recessive orders such as cystic fibrosis, sickle cell anaemia, betathalassemia and Tay-Sachs. Carrier screening places adults in the awkward position as to whether they should procreate knowing they will pass on their defective genes.

5 **Pre-symptomatic**: this can be done at any age especially for late onset of diseases such Alzheimer's and Huntington's and also for predispositions such as to heart disease and cancer. This form of screening is problematic as early diagnosis can cause a great psychological burden especially as there is not much that can be done for these diseases at the moment.

a) Mandatory and voluntary screening

Key question

Should screening be made compulsory?

Key word

Mandatory means compulsory under law.

A major debate in many countries is whether screening should be **mandatory** or voluntary. The debate is essentially utilitarian.

The arguments for mandatory screening are:

- early detection of abnormality reduces pain both for parents and future persons
- provides better informed choices for prospective parents
- fewer defects in children if selection takes place (e.g. at pre-implantation stage)
- reduction in financial costs in care of the disabled which would then provide more funds for other health issues
- removes potentially less productive people from society
- reduces trauma of early deaths through early diagnosis
- encourages adults only to give birth to healthy people.

The arguments against mandatory screening and in favour of voluntary screening are:

- erosion of democratic values such as liberty and personal choice
- it can cause feelings of hopelessness because of the lack of treatments (such as Huntington's and Alzheimer's diseases)
- it causes discrimination towards those detected with diseases or who are carriers
- it can cause worry and unjustified relief to those with misdiagnosis
- some feel that there is a great deal of social pressure to abort foetuses or discard pre-embryos which are abnormal.

Key question

Should a person with genetic abnormalities be obliged to tell his family and employers?

b) Knowledge and confidentiality

These arguments for mandatory and voluntary screening both pose a fundamental problem of what one does with the genetic knowledge once it is gained. This question has personal as well as wider social implications.

There is much debate amongst **feminist** writers about the use of screening pre-implantation or in the womb. Some argue that knowing whether the foetus is healthy or not is vital for a woman's autonomy as it is she who will become the primary carer and so the decision whether to discard an embryo or have an abortion should be hers. A more radical line is that it is not in the best interests of the embryo to be born severely disabled and that it would be better to bring a healthy child into the world who can have all the benefits of a mother who really wants it. This view worries other feminists. Selection of this kind sounds strongly like eugenics, a patriarchal notion that there is only one perfect kind of human being (and society). The feminist writer Adrienne Asch, for example, argues that there is a great deal of difference between having an abortion because a woman finds herself abandoned and not wanting a child because it has a limb deformity. She points out how many feminists are incensed if abortion takes place because the child is the wrong sex but see no problem if it has another kind of 'defect'. She argues that feminists should be as worried about 'ableism' as about sexism.

The feminist arguments suggest that maybe sometimes it is best not to know what the sex or possible abnormalities of the baby are and to deal with the child whatever its characteristics.

However, the problem of what to do with genetic knowledge once it is gained is especially problematic if it has implications for others. For example should a person who has been diagnosed with Huntington's disease be under an obligation to tell other close members of the family so that they can be screened or should they be allowed to keep this information to themselves? We have looked at the ethical problems of **confidentiality** in Chapter 1 but there are serious practical implications posed by genetic screening:

Cross-reference

Read pages 6–9 for a fuller discussion on the issues of confidentiality.

- **Insurance companies.** Would a person be obliged to divulge to an insurance company the results of any screenings that he had undergone? It would make sense, especially for other non-afflicted insurance holders, that those predisposed towards genetic disorders should pay more on their insurance premiums because they will cost the insurance companies more in health care in the future. It seems unfair that those who *know* they are genetically diseased should pay the same insurance money as those who are not genetically diseased.

- **Employers**. Letting an employer know about a disease might be in everyone's best interest, but ignorance about genetic disorders is often as great as misinformation about HIV or AIDS and can be used against a person. Unless there could be an enforceable 'genetic discrimination' law then information will inevitably remain confidential which might not be to everyone's advantage.

- **Family**. In many countries having a blood test is a pre-condition of marriage but what information should be passed on to a future partner? Such tests also depend on the accuracy and sensitivity of detecting certain diseases, besides which it might be argued that a relationship depends on dealing with whatever life throws at one; knowing that a person might develop a crippling condition could distort a normal healthy lifestyle. But what should be done if a person develops a condition (for example breast cancer) which if known about early could be treated successfully but who refuses to tell other family members? Would it be right for a doctor, having tried to gain voluntary consent, and judging that the lack of information would cause considerable harm, to break the confidence? The instrumental or consequentialist view appears reasonable, but it still leaves open just how to judge 'serious harm'. The deontologist who considers fidelity and trust to be paramount in the doctor–patient relationship also has a duty for the health care of others. It is for this reason (see page 8 above) that Beauchamp and Childress argued that duties cannot be absolute but prima facie, and that even the deontologist has to act according to the situation.

5 The use of stem cells

The use of **stem cells** offers science the very great opportunity of treating life-threatening diseases by programming cells to replace defective cells. Stem cells are cells which have no defined role and can be found throughout the body. The body needs them to replace defective or damaged cells.

Stem cells fall into two kinds: embryonic stem cells (ESC) and adult stem cells (ASC). The real distinction is not so much whether the cells are found in an embryo or adult (ASC can, for example, be found in embryos) but how they function.

- **Totipotent (or pluripotent) stem cells** are cells which have the potential to be programmed into any kind of body cell/tissue. They are usually found at the **embryonic stage** in the inner cells of the blastocyst and extracted after nine days after fertilisation (at the 100–200 cell stage). This cannot be done without destroying the embryo.

- **Multipotent stem cells** or adult stem cells can be found in bone marrow, heart muscle, umbilical cord blood and placenta. AS cells have a smaller range of functions but their natural role is to replace damaged tissues or treat diseases such as leukaemia. They are therefore less 'plastic' than ES cells.

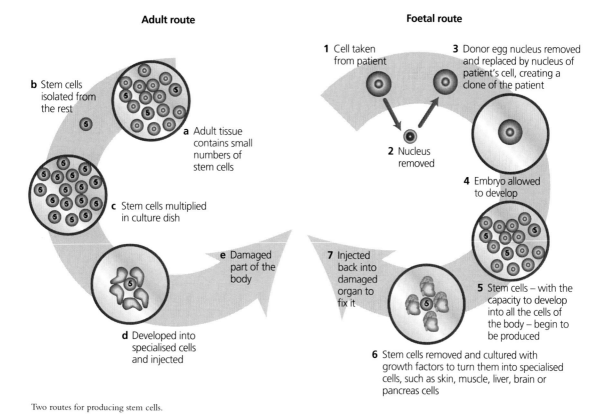

Two routes for producing stem cells.

Key quote

It is relatively easy to grow an entire plant from a small cutting, something which seems inconceivable in humans. Yet this study brings us tantalisingly close to using types of skin cells to grow many different types of human tissues.

AZIM SURANI, CAMBRIDGE UNIVERSITY, *THE TIMES*, 21 NOVEMBER 2007

There are two main moral problems of using stem cells. The first is that using totipotent (ES) stem cells means that the developing embryo has to be destroyed to harvest the stem cells. The second problem is the risks involved by reprogramming multipotent cells (AS) so as to get them to 'forget' their previous role. The body produces a stem cell for every cell with a defined role but not all AS cells behave in the same way and some reprogrammed stem cells can revert back to their earlier state but in an uncontrolled way. So instead of being able to cure a patient's defective tissue the uncontrolled cells become tumours. In one case the tumour bowel cancer cells were found to be made up of teeth, hair and toe-nail cells. The challenge for scientists is to zero adult stem cells to behave like ES cells.

Summary diagram

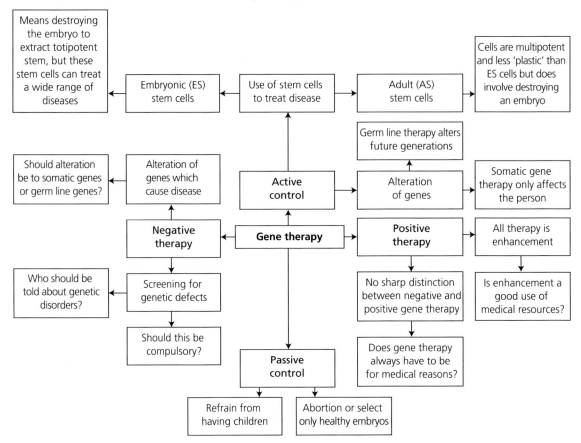

6 Normative ethical responses to gene therapy and the use of stem cells

Key question

Should there be limits to medical research?

a) Consequentialism

From a **consequentialist** moral position where there is doubt about the status of the pre-embryo, the aim must be to find AS cells which are totipotent. Very recently some scientists claim to have been able to get skin cells to behave as ES cells through **induced pluripotent stem (IPS) cells**. But there is no certainty at the moment that these cells won't mutate and form tumours. In addition consequentialists also consider the risk and benefits of somatic and germ line therapies.

i) Act utilitarians

Act utilitarian consequentialists offer the following considerations in the use of stem cells:

- Patients using AS cells have to be aware of the risks of making their conditions worse.

- Success rates of IPS at the moment are very low (1 in 5,000 cells in one recent case) but it might be worth gambling that in a particular case it might turn out well.
- By using IPS and improving scientific knowledge the chances for long-term success and happiness are greatly improved.
- There is still a need to harvest ES cells as a model on which to develop IPS cells. However, the greater good justifies the necessary destruction of pre-embryos.
- As ES cells are not persons or sentient beings and as no pain or harm is caused, and no interests/preferences are denied, then the destruction of the embryo is not morally relevant.

ii) Welfare utilitarians

Welfare utilitarian consequentialists offer the following responses to act utilitarian objections to the use of **germ line cell therapy**:

Cross-reference

For the aims of welfare utilitarians see page 29 above.

- In response to the criticism that it is far less risky to use somatic therapy as it affects only one person not many, the welfare utilitarian responds that although there are risks these are comparatively small and far outweighed by the welfare benefits which have the potential to rid society of many dangerous diseases. It would also cut down on the considerable cost of all future somatic treatments for many generations to come.
- In response to the criticism that germ-line therapy affects all future generations who will not have had the opportunity to consent to such radical alteration of their genes, welfare utilitarians argue that parents make welfare choices about their children from the start. Furthermore, as it is impossible to get permission from future generations it is not a good reason to ban it; we make all kinds of decisions which affect future generations without making consent an issue. The guiding principle for the welfare utilitarian might be, 'if it is good for this generation then it is good enough for future generations'.
- Some fear that germ-line therapy could be driven by a political ideology and used as a eugenic device to create a new superior kind of society but the welfare utilitarian considers this to be scaremongering and suggests that we should be more concerned by those who use their money to buy medical technology for their own selfish ends when they could be using their wealth for the general welfare of society in other ways.

Cross-reference

Refer back to Chapter 2 on the problems of personhood and sanctity of life.

However, for many the **deontological** command to respect the embryo is still a major determining factor in the ES cell debate. It is the primary reason why experimentation on foetuses and the use of all ES cells is forbidden in some legislation (in the USA, for example).

b) Natural law

Natural law deontologists hold the view that innocent human life should always be protected. In the modern Roman Catholic Church teaching an innocent life is considered to come into existence at the moment of conception. The Church uses the Aristotelian distinction between being a potential and actual person. The embryo as a potential person will, all things being equal, become a person or persons and should therefore be given the dignity and respect of a person. Singer's argument is rejected on the grounds that, however many persons the blastocyst *might* become, there is still a duty to protect all innocent life at whatever stage it might be.

However, some have argued that some blastocysts naturally stop developing at a few days old. In this case it would be reasonable to use ES cells as their removal would not be killing an embryo which has no vital organs, no brain and no potential to become a human being. The Roman Catholic Church rejects this argument because this only treats the physical aspect of the embryo. An embryo, like all human beings, is a **psychosomatic** whole and it cannot be said for certain that a body has no 'soul' unless it is dead. Pope John Paul II stated:

> *Therefore at no moment in its development can the embryo be the sub-ject of tests that are not beneficial or of experimentation that would inevitably lead to its destruction or mutilation or irreversibly damage it, for man's nature itself would be mocked and wounded.*
>
> (John Paul II, *Society Must Protect Embryos*, address to a working party on the legal and clinical aspects of the Human Genome Project, 1993)

The Catholic natural law tradition, however, does not reject all gene therapy if it is for 'strictly therapeutic' reasons and its aim is to ameliorate the genetic disorder (an aim which is not contrary to Aquinas' primary principle of self preservation, progress and reproduction) providing that it is for the well-being of the person and not for positive or cosmetic reasons. The Church states that it is therefore wrong to change aspects of a person which are:

> *not found on the integral reality of the human person, at the risk of doing damage to his dignity. In this case it exposes man to the caprice of others, by depriving him of his autonomy...*
>
> (John Paul II, *Ethics of Genetic Manipulation*)

This ambiguous statement suggests that gene therapy which deliberately causes genetic handicap (as in the treatment of very early embryos) or which is done without a person's consent for 'capricious' or trivial reasons (for cosmetic reasons such as sex or looks) is intrinsically wrong. In summary the Catholic natural law teaches that:

- as all IVF procedures separate procreative and unitive sex then all gene therapies which occur pre-implantation and outside the womb are wrong;
- all procedures which deliberately produce spare foetuses are wrong;
- embryo selection for therapeutic reasons is wrong as it entails killing some foetuses;
- genetic enhancement is wrong if it is for cosmetic reasons, although the alteration of a gene which causes excessive aggressive behaviour (for example) might be possible;
- germ-line enhancement is usually wrong because of the risks involved and because we do not have the *same* kind of duties to future generations.

Helen Watt expresses it as follows:

> *We do not have the same responsibilities for strangers (i.e. future generations) as we do for ourselves and for our children. Just as it would be intrusive for the State to take children off the street and put braces on their teeth, it would be similarly intrusive (and in practice far too dangerous) to attempt a non-therapeutic change to germ-line).*

(Helen Watt, *Explaining Catholic Teaching: Gene Therapy*, page 44)

c) Revealed ethics

Revealed law deontologists who hold an absolutist conservative position express this in terms of the **strong sanctity of life argument**. The Bible supports the vitalist notion that life begins at conception and that innocent life should always be protected, for the same reasons that all forms of abortion are intrinsically wrong. However, supporters of **weak sanctity of life** arguments consider that the reasons why abortion may be rejected are different from the use of ES cells. In the case of abortion there are other, second-order considerations such as the value of motherhood, sexuality and sexual responsibility which put together usually present a case against abortion. But as none of those factors are relevant here, then the good achieved through the use of ES may be the most loving thing to do as it offers a greater quality of life to future generations.

The outspoken and influential Protestant theologian **Paul Ramsey** (1913–1988) warned in his influential book *Fabricated Man* (1970) against the development of technology which would fail to treat human life with the dignity which it deserves. Even though many of the risks he envisaged have not occurred, the principles which Ramsey established cut across theological and secular thinking.

- As **co-creators** with God we have a duty of care to create and maintain the world.
- If there is to be a genetic defect in a child then the only ethical form of genetic control must be **passive**, that is, to *refrain* from

procreation. Theologically the use of sterilisation 'may be morally obligatory'. In fact if Christians have a duty to bring healthy children into the world, then they should also see it as their *duty* to remain celibate.

- Active genetic control is not acceptable. Whereas the utilitarian scientist might argue that if the human 'machinery' is defective it should be improved, Ramsey considered the purpose of creation is to enable a relationship of love between humans and God. Thus he preferred the term 'procreation' (creating as God does through love) rather than 'reproduction' (mechanical). His major objection was against the use of cloning.

- Genetic engineering symbolises the **domination of technology** over *ourselves*. It destroys human relationships based on love and co-operation. Technology of this kind is a form of divorce which 'puts asunder' what God and humans create through loving sexual relationships. The real risk is that what we create might *not* be good, but rather a series of appalling blunders which cannot be morally or theologically justified.

Ramsey's approach indicates a range of possible Christian responses. For many Protestants decisions have to be made based on the three-fold relationship between revelation (Bible), reason (knowledge of the natural world) and tradition (the teaching of the Church). Decisions ultimately depend on **conscience** and personal responsibility. For example the Anglican authors of *Personal Origins* (1996) argue that as stewards of the natural order we have a role to develop the potentials of the created order. Parents therefore who remove *serious* genetic defects are acting in a far more loving and responsible way than parents who have children and then either divorce or separate. The question of germ-line therapy will depend on what science may reasonably predict.

d) Kantian ethics

Kantian deontologists might argue from two positions. The first might be that as I would not have wanted to be experimented upon or discarded as an embryo, I would therefore not wish it to happen to others. Therefore, through the categorical imperative it now becomes a universal duty to protect all embryonic human life. The first position is reinforced by the second (the practical imperative) position that as it is never right to treat people as a means to an end, but an end in themselves, then the use of ES cells should be rejected as it treats the early embryo as a resource to be cannibalised and not as a person.

However, the fundamental problem with the Kantian position is highlighted by the third version of the imperative which is that in the kingdom of ends everyone is a law-maker whose decisions take into account all other human beings as law-makers. But the status of the early embryo could hardly enable it to be considered to be a rational,

Key quote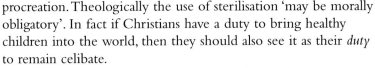

Men ought not to play God before they learn to be men, and after they have learned to be men, they will not play God.

PAUL RAMSEY, *FABRICATED MAN*, PAGE 138

Cross-reference

Read pages 21–23 above for the aims and principles of Kantian ethics.

even sentient, member of the kingdom of ends. A Kantian might argue for the protection of the weak but, as the early embryo displays no rational features at all, then it ceases to be a matter of moral concern.

e) Virtue ethics

Virtue ethicists have a significant role to play in the process and application of medicine. This is clearly expressed in the Human Fertilisation and Embryology Act (1990), which states the following:

1 *It shall be the duty of the individual under whose supervision the activities authorised by a licence are carried on (referred to in this Act as the 'person responsible') to secure –*
   a *that the other persons to whom the licence applies are of such character, and are so qualified by training and experience, as to be suitable persons to participate in the activities authorised by the licence,*
   b *that proper equipment is used,*
   c *that proper arrangements are made for the keeping of gametes and embryos and for the disposal of gametes or embryos that have been allowed to perish,*
   d *that suitable practices are used in the course of the activities, and*
   e *that the conditions of the licence are complied with.*

   (*The Human Fertilisation and Embryology Act,*
   1990, Chapter 1, paragraph 17)

The Act therefore states the fundamentally important principle of medicine that the scientists and physicians involved in the sensitive issues of ES cell research can be trusted to work within the limits of the law and public expectation. This is not easy and requires the skill or *phronesis* of balancing the desire to push forward the boundaries of medical knowledge but within the constraints of law, good practice and the welfare of patients. The virtue ethicist therefore counsels the virtue of caution; somatic cell treatment should in the first instance be preferred over germ-line therapy so that the consequences of somatic therapy can be properly assessed.

The virtue ethicist is also concerned with the way in which knowledge is imparted to the community. Doctors and scientists have a duty to ensure that claims of success are not exaggerated and that the public aren't led to think that gene therapy offers a wonder cure and that diseases such as Alzheimer's or Huntington's can now suddenly be cured.

The virtue ethicist reminds doctors and scientists alike that the development of gene therapy, like all scientific progress, must be done openly and honestly not only within the community of the medical profession but within the scrutiny of the wider community (i.e. the *polis*). Virtue ethics has an important **performative** function (see page 5 above) in putting together ethical committees made up of various members of society who represent different ethical interests. Committees therefore have to practise the skill of balancing diverse ethical principles with the virtues of perseverance, humility and integrity.

Finally the virtue ethicist might consider whether positive therapy as enhancement is really for human flourishing or whether it is excessive and in some ways exploitative of others or unfair. As we have seen, the virtue ethicist might judge that the parent who selects various genes at the pre-embryo stage to be just as bad as the over-pushy parent who sends their child to extra music lessons after school in order to become a concert pianist.

Study guide

By the end of this chapter, you should have considered different types of genetic manipulation and the reasons for their usage. You should be aware of the controversy of so-called 'designer' babies but more particularly the ambiguity over the term 'genetic enhancement' and use of different types of stem cells. In addition you should be able to outline the moral problems involved with genetic screening, knowledge and confidentiality. You should be able to apply the various normative ethical systems to all these issues.

Revision checklist

Can you explain the difference between:

- negative and positive gene therapy
- passive and active genetic control
- germ line cell therapy and somatic gene cell therapy
- totipotent stem cells and multipotent stem cells
- embryonic (ES) stem cells, adult (AS) stem cells and induced pluripotent stem (IPS) cells
- strong and weak sanctity of life approach to gene therapy.

Can you name the connection to the issue of gene therapy of each of the following:

- Thomas Murray
- Paul Ramsey
- Julian Savulescu
- Pope John Paul II.

Can you give arguments for and against:

- the Roman Catholic natural law rejection of therapeutic gene therapy
- the act and welfare utilitarian position on gene therapy and stem cells
- the Kantian position of an embryo's right to moral consideration
- who should have access to genetic knowledge.

Essay question

1a. Explain the reasons for human genetic therapy as enhancement.

1b. 'The only reason for using gene therapy is to cure diseases.' Discuss.

An essay might begin by explaining the term 'human genetic therapy'. It may then develop this explanation by noting that not all treatment is regarded as enhancement as some argue that, although negative gene therapy is justified, positive gene therapy is not. Enhancement might be justified on the grounds that there are many things which improve a person's existence; these might include education, better food and a more stimulating environment. The enhancement arguments might dismiss objections on the grounds that drawing a line between positive and negative gene therapy is arbitrary, that the ends (happiness) justify the means, that it is a matter of individual autonomy how we treat our bodies and, finally, the 'Promethean' argument that it is impossible not to use technology in this way.

The evaluative element of this essay should tackle some of the propositions set out in 1a, namely that arbitrariness is not irrational and the fact that something is possible doesn't make it right. Normative systems which might support this view might include the revealed ethical position which supports the notion that intentions that are based purely on vanity or cosmetic reasons should be rejected and only identifiable diseases should be treated. On the other hand discussion might take into account the fact that humans are social beings and therefore being able to live in a community suggests that whereas being aggressive may be acceptable in one group it may be regarded as a defect in another. A virtue ethical response may be helpful in this context.

Further essay questions

2a Explain how virtue ethics affects how gene therapy is performed.
2b Assess the view that virtue ethics provides very little help in the issues raised by gene therapy.

3 'Genetic screening should be made compulsory.' Discuss.

4 To what extent does utilitarianism provide the most coherent ethical approach to the use of human stem cells in medicine?

1 Organ transplant dilemmas

Case study

Dr Shann's dilemma

Dr Frank Shann, director of the Melbourne Royal Children's Hospital intensive care unit, was presented in 1989 with the following dilemma of two babies in his unit.

- Baby A, a boy, was suffering from a severe heart disease and having suffered several heart attacks was placed on a ventilator and given a continuous supply of drugs to keep him alive.
- In all other respects Baby A was normal, but because of the heart disease, his situation was described as 'hopeless'.
- Baby B, in the adjacent bed, had been well until he suffered 'catastrophic collapse'. He had abnormal blood vessels in the brain which had suddenly collapsed causing blood to flow into the brain, destroying the cerebral cortex. But his brain stem was functioning enough to keep him alive on a ventilator and sufficient not to pronounce him legally dead.

- As it happened, both babies had the same blood group and it would have been possible to transplant the heart of Baby B to aid Baby A.
- But under Australian law, as Baby B was still legally alive there was nothing Dr Shann could do. As a result both babies died.

(cited in Peter Singer, *Rethinking Life and Death*, pages 38–42)

This dilemma for Dr Shann was that, as a good doctor, he had the means of saving at least one life through heart transplantation but it would have meant deliberately killing one baby without its consent. But whose consent is needed? Could the parents have given it? Another problem is how death is to be defined. Although Baby B was alive in one sense some argue that the technology which kept him alive was in fact masking the fact that he was really dead.

Key word

Transplantation means removing an organ and replanting it or re-establishing it in someone else.

Organ transplantation in its modern form began in 1954 when a kidney from a living donor was successfully transplanted to a patient. Before this time skin and bone grafts had been carried out from the mid-nineteenth century, and blood transfusions and cornea transplants from the beginning of the twentieth century. However, what made this kidney transfer possible was that the donor was from a close relative and so the problem of the body's rejection of the alien organ was largely overcome. But the use of **Cyclosporin**, a powerful immune inhibitor, in 1978 transformed organ transplantations. Cyclosporin (and other similar drugs) enable non-family members to donate organs with a greatly increased chance that the patient's body will not reject the new organ for many years, if not indefinitely.

Since the 1970s transplants of whole 'functional organs' such as heart, liver, lungs, intestines and pancreas have all been developed successfully. Other transplants such as skin, corneas, bone marrow, blood cells, blood vessels and heart valves have also been transplanted but as these are parts of organs the ethical issues are not quite the same.

Kidney transplants are by far the most common transplants followed by liver transplants. The ethical issues raised by organ transplantation are:

- receiving an organ as a patient
- taking organs from dead bodies/donors
- giving organs from live donors
- paying for organs
- finding new sources of organs.

2 The law and organ transplantation

The **Human Tissue Act** (2004) forbids commercial organ donation and maintains the important principle that all human organs and tissues must be given voluntarily. The regulation of the use of organs and tissues is controlled by the **Human Tissue Authority** (HTA).

The relevant aspects of the Act for organ transplantation state the following:

- **Consent.** Full or, as the Act calls it, 'appropriate' consent is required by live donors and donors may make consent in writing for use of their organs after death. Family members may not overrule those who have registered their desire for their organs to be used at death.
- **Regulation.** The HTA controls the use of all organs from live and deceased donors either for transplantation or for other anatomical investigation. This includes the import and export of organs. The HTA grants licences to those individuals carrying out organ and tissue transplantations, storing and disposal of body parts and anatomical investigations.
- **Trafficking.** It is illegal to receive, supply or enter negotiations in order to buy or sell organs from dead bodies. Punishment may include imprisonment up to three years or a fine or both.
- **Organs from live persons.** It is illegal to take an organ from a live person who has not given appropriate consent and who has not been given the appropriate information about the nature and risks of transplantation. A person commits an offence when he 'knowingly or recklessly supplies information which is false or misleading in a material respect'.

a) Presumed consent

Key thought

Presumed consent in law means that a person's consent to have their organs removed at death is assumed to have been given unless an adult has expressly indicated otherwise.

The Human Tissue Act (2004) specifically rejects presumed consent. However, due to the great shortage of organ donations some countries have changed their laws to presume consent so that at death doctors may lawfully remove organs for transplantation, unless a person has specifically stated that they wish to opt out. There are two versions of presumed consent: 'soft opt-out' allows relatives to refuse organ transplantation and 'hard opt-out' which does not allow relatives any opinion.

The following gives some examples of the law in various countries at present.

- The **UK** at present has no presumed consent. People may place their names on the NHS Organ Donor Register.
- **Spain** has a soft opt-out system where, if the dead person has not previously opted out themselves, their relatives may deny consent for organ donation on the person's behalf.

- **Austria** has a hard opt-out system which ignores the views of relatives and the dead person is presumed to have given consent.

b) Required consent

The **USA** has a different system of '**required request**'. The law states 'that it shall be illegal as well as irresponsible to disconnect a ventilator from an individual who's declared dead following brain stem testing without first making proper enquiry as to the possibility of that individual's tissues and organs being used for the purposes of transplantation'.

3 Receiving an organ

The aim of transplant surgery is, of course, to restore to health a sick patient with a functioning organ which replaces the diseased or damaged organ. In many cases a transplant can save a life and in others (such as a cornea replacement) it can significantly improve the quality of life of the patient. Tens of thousands of people every year have their lives extended and enhanced through organ replacement.

The arguments against transplantation are a combination of risks (physical and psychological) and cost.

- A patient might have psychological problems with the sex or race of the donor.
- A patient might feel very awkward taking the organs of a very young person killed in an accident.
- A patient might feel overwhelmed, even guilty, receiving such a generous gift of an organ in what has been termed as the 'tyranny of the gift'.
- Patients have also to realise that not all transplants work and that in some cases transplants can fail when the body even four or five years later then rejects the organ.
- The cost of finding and performing transplant surgery has to be balanced against the health gains. In some less acute cases **dialysis** may be a preferable option to organ replacement.
- The use of drugs required to reduce rejection by the body can cause other diseases.

> **Key word**
>
> **Dialysis** is the process by which a machine can perform the task of the defective organ (usually a kidney).

4 Dead donors

One source of organs is from dead bodies. This has the obvious advantage that a dead person has no need for their organs and with their advance consent (for example by carrying a donor card or by expressing it in a will) transplant surgery can use organs to help others.

A key ethical code in all organ transplantation is that a doctor or
physician should never deliberately kill their patients even if requested
to do so. The **dead donor rule** therefore forbids taking the organs
from a donor until death can be properly established. However, this
presents the doctors and surgeons with a number of problems.

Firstly, organs work better if taken immediately from the dead
person. The longer organs remain in the dead person's body the
more they will deteriorate (due to lack of oxygen) and become less
effective.

Secondly, being able to control the moment of death enables
doctors the time to prepare the receiving patient for surgery. This
might mean keeping someone alive a little longer or indeed
reducing the length of their life.

Finally, the dead donor rule depends on the patient giving their
consent for the use of body parts. This can cause delays and reduce
the number of organs which are desperately needed for ill patients.

a) Defining death

The solution to the first two problems is to reconsider what is
meant by death, the issue posed by the example of Dr Shann's
dilemma at the start of this chapter. The traditional view of **body
death** was defined as lack of breathing, lack of heart-beat and no
response to stimuli (for example pupils do not dilate when light is
shone into them).

However, in more recent years it has become more common to
talk of **brain death** as the determining factor that the person is now
dead. In the UK the definition is even more specific and given as
brain stem dead (the brain stem is the lower part of the brain
without which the brain cannot operate).

Both definitions, the body death view and the brain death view,
have been used as reasons to take organs but both views have met
with considerable opposition.

- **Brain dead** diagnosis of death could suggest in the case of a
  patient in a persistent vegetative state (PVS) that, even though the
  body is 'alive' perhaps through artificial means, the person has
  died because there is no brain activity. The use of life support
  machinery has disguised death and therefore taking organs from a
  body which is still operating is not killing it. For those who hold
  a **dualist** view of body and personhood, once the brain ceases to
  function then even if the body is alive through its own means the
  person no longer exists. However, both these views put too much
  emphasis on the brain as the main source of personhood when
  for many death has to include the total disintegration of mind
  and body which is also *irreversible*. There have been many cases of
  PVS patients who have made remarkable recoveries.

- **Body death** diagnosis has the advantage that for many people death is clearly indicated by the more traditional view that a body which is stiff and cold is no longer alive. The brain dead definition has the difficult emotional problem that organs may be taken from a body where heart and lungs are still operating. But the body death definition also has its problems as the celebrated **Pittsburgh Protocol** (1993) case illustrates. The Pittsburgh clinic, using the traditional body view, was removing organs two minutes after death. However, they were making no attempts to recover heart beat and other technologies were being ignored to recover a life. What shocked the public was that the dying patient appeared to have been given lower priority than the patient in need of an organ. The protocol was abandoned due to public pressure.

The only safe conclusion is that death has to be a combination of both body and brain death.

b) Defining consent

Key question

Is it right to have a law based on presumed consent which allows doctors to take organs from those who have died for transplantation?

However, even if the more stringent definition of death is adopted, demand for organs far outstrips supply and, even when a person has given consent for their organs to be used when they die, it sometimes happens that family members refuse to let this happen. Over 500,000 people carry donor cards in the UK, but this is not enough to meet demand. The problem of organ supply could be solved immediately if the government introduced **presumed consent** as practised in France, Spain and Austria. If a person does not want to be a donor, it is then a matter of declining consent by removing themselves from the donor list.

But presumed consent dislodges the lynchpin of organ donorship which is that the giving of organs should be an autonomous and therefore freely consenting act. Presumed consent could be considered to presume too much, especially in the emotionally sensitive area of death. Critics of presumed consent accuse it of paternalism and undue interference from the state which undermines the key value of a liberal democracy, that of self-determination.

5 Live donors

The use of live donors overcomes many of the problems of dead donors. The advantages are that the time and place of organ transfer from donor to recipient patient can be planned and the conditions established for the best care for donor, patient and organ.

a) Physical risks

The physical risks to donors are:

- death, although recent research indicates that for over ten years this has been about 0.03 per cent (for kidney donors) and 0.23 per cent for life-threatening conditions and complications
- harm caused by surgery such as pain, infection, blood clots and reaction to anaesthetics. For **liver transplants** the risk of donor liver failure and mortality since 1987 is 0.2 per cent.
- change in lifestyle (i.e. due to loss of a kidney).

b) The problem of causing harm to live donors

All organ transplants cause deliberate harm to the donor with no obvious *medical* welfare advantage. **Non-maleficence** poses a fundamental problem for doctors' ethical codes which state that a doctor should never cause direct harm to his patient, nor use surgery for anything other than the welfare of the patient.

However, by common consensus modern practice has accepted the principle that, if a person wishes to exercise their autonomy over their body to donate freely an organ to another person with no direct damage to their health and for the medical benefit of another person, then they have a just reason for inflicting short-term harm (through surgery and the period of recovery afterwards). Kidney donation is permissible because it is possible to live a healthy lifestyle on the remaining kidney, and liver and even lung lobe donations are acceptable because the donor's body is able to regenerate the missing organ part.

However, as a matter of course, the doctor must advise on the risks and what is in the donor's own **best interests**. He might, for example, point out alternative treatment for the patient (such as dialysis) and drugs or alternative sources of organs (such as animals). He will also advise on whether the donor's organ is suitable for transplantation (i.e. it is not diseased or incompatible). However, there are a number of issues which test these conditions.

- **Coercion.** Some have argued that, as many donors are family members, there will be undue pressure on the weakest member of the family to become a donor (i.e. the one who is not married, has no children as dependants) which would make it very difficult for them not to consent. However, there is very little evidence this is so and most people express their pleasure at being able to help another.
- **Indirect coercion.** Another form of coercion is when a person is emotionally coerced by the sense that they have a duty to be a donor. For example a father may feel that if he doesn't give a liver lobe to his sick child, then he will be judged a bad parent by

Key word

Live donor **liver transplants** began in 1987 and consist of taking a liver lobe from the donor and transplanting it in the recipient. The lost lobe should grow back again.

Key question

Is it right for doctors to cause physical harm to people for no direct medical benefit?

Key word

Non-maleficence is one of the four basic principles of doctors' ethics (the others being autonomy, beneficence and justice). Read page 6 above.

Key quote

A physician shall act only in the patient's interest when providing medical care which might have the effect of weakening the physical and mental condition of the patient.
THE DECLARATION OF GENEVA, A MODERN VERSION OF THE HIPPOCRATIC OATH BY THE WORLD MEDICAL ASSOCIATION

Key question

Should a doctor accept an organ from a donor even if the donor dies as a consequence?

Key word

Altruism is a free and generous act for others.

society (or his family). Some however argue that this is not coercion but rather a genuine sense of love or compassion which hasn't reduced a person's autonomy but is in fact informing it.

- **Heroic donors.** How should a doctor behave when a person offers their organ for transplant against all medical advice – that is, the donation might kill the donor, or the organ might be unsuitable? The dilemma for the doctor is that he has already accepted a broadened notion of welfare which accepts that being a donor is part of his welfare duty. However, in this case the donor's actions will clearly be very harmful. Some argue that the doctor must act in the donor's best interest and refuse the donation, even though this means acting paternally and disrespecting his autonomy. Others suggest that as the principle of live donors has been accepted, then having given the donor all the medical facts, it must be the responsibility of the donor to act autonomously even if this is entirely against the doctor's advice. Of course there is no guarantee that the heroic donor's wishes may be carried out as the surgeon performing the organ transfer may refuse to do so.

- **Strangers as donors.** Whereas many live donors are family members who have a psychological justification for donating an organ, donation by strangers poses some additional ethical problems. If causing harm to donors (through surgery) is problematic for family members, it is even harder to justify causing harm to a complete stranger, who has no psychological direct emotional attachment to the patient. The question for many depends on whether **altruism** is sufficient reason to allow harm to non-family donors by doctors. This is a significant point because the definition of donor appears to rest on an act of generosity, but critics wonder whether a stranger might in fact have other motives for their action which would question their genuineness. However, for others what matters is not altruism but a well-informed and **autonomous act** which has not been coerced, but the problem with this concession is that it allows for payment for live donor organs which in many people's minds is morally unacceptable (see below).

6 Commercial aspects of organ transplantation

a) Paying donors for organs

In most countries paying for organs from donors is considered to be a violation of the notion of donorship which considers that the giving of an organ should be a free and generous act without financial gain. In most countries, therefore, it is illegal to buy and sell organs from living and deceased donors.

Some of the arguments against paying for organs from donors often include:

Cross-reference

See pages 67–68 above on the reasons against slavery.

- It is a form of slavery and demeans the value of people by placing a price on their bodies. It puts a price on the priceless.
- It reduces the value of altruism and society's dependency on acts of generosity from its members.
- It might exploit the poor by unscrupulous businesses hoping to make a profit out of the great demand for organs.
- It shows no respect for the dead when a body might be sold off for its organs.

But are these arguments really persuasive? Ronald Munson argues that they all appear to be based on an understanding of altruism and respect for persons where what is really at stake is respect for autonomy and there is no logical reason why the commercial sale of organs should undermine this. The main objections to the sale of organs are consequential, such as putting pressure on poor people to sell their organs, but this could be controlled by law and international protocols.

> *If the autonomy of the individual is the basis for recognizing that, when the conditions of informed consent are met, donating a kidney to some- one is a morally legitimate act it must also be morally legitimate for the individual to be paid for donating the kidney.*
> (Ronald Munson, *Oxford Handbook of Bioethics*, page 226)

He rejects the slavery view because the sale of an organ is not the sale of the whole person, nor can this show disrespect for other members of society by undermining or harming their autonomy. However, from a consequentialist view it is possible that the commercialisation of organs could lead to the exploitation of the poor. But this does not make the sale of organs intrinsically wrong.

b) Costs and deciding on the most deserving cases

Key question

Should an alcoholic be just as deserving of a liver transplant as a non-alcoholic person with a diseased liver?

Cross-reference

Read pages 9–12 above on the ethical problems of distribution of resources.

The lack of organs causes particular problems for medicine. How do doctors determine which are the deserving cases? For example does a young person have more of a case for an organ transplant than an old person? In addition, the expense of one organ transplantation (the cost of the transfer, the expenses incurred because of the surgery needed to extract and place the organ and the aftercare needed for a single patient and donor) could be considered to be less persuasive than treating many other people.

Should someone who has consistently smoked or drunk too much against medical advice have just as much a case as someone who through misfortune suffered organ failure or disease? Recent proposals in the National Health Service suggest setting up a contract between patients and the NHS which require those who are overweight or smoke to make lifestyle changes first before an operation. The contract, therefore, does not make treatment an automatic right but requires the patient and the NHS to understand the relationship between their respective rights and responsibilities.

Finally, when making decisions it has sometimes to be reckoned that living longer or having added years is not necessarily a good thing. Quality of life has to be a balance of being able to act on desires as well as having time and opportunity to live them out. Sometimes it might be reckoned that enjoying the life that is left is more worthwhile than risky, painful and uncertain surgery.

7 Alternative organ sources

If pigs' organs and genetic composition are very close to humans' should they be used as a source of organs for humans? This image is taken from the BBC series *Pig Heart Boy*, about a boy who receives a pig's heart to replace his own faulty heart.

Key word

Xenotransplantation is cross-animal organ transfer.

In order to overcome some of the ethical problems of live and dead donorship it might be possible in the future to use mechanical hearts, lungs, etc. But this technology is still in its very early days. There is also the possibility of using stem cells and cloning (which is discussed in the next chapter).

a) Xenotransplantation

Another source of organs and tissues is from animals. **Xenotransplantation** offers a ready supply of organs if genetically modified (to reduce rejection by human bodies).

In 1997 the **United Kingdom Xenotransplantation Interim Regulation Authority** (UKXIRA) was established to advise the government of xenotransplantation in humans. On a practical level the authority has to ensure that viruses are not transferred from animals to humans, or that a transfer doesn't create a new disease. It also has to consider whether, for example, transferring a pig's heart to a human is too risky (the organ may introduce viruses into humans which, like the AIDS virus, could have devastating effects).

b) Moral arguments against xenotransplantation

Moral arguments against xenotransplantation might include:

- It is wrong to exploit animals without their consent for human use; it is a form of speciesism.
- Animals and humans belong to different aspects of the created order; using animals for their organs disorders the natural purpose of animals and humans in nature.
- Only non-reproductive organs may be used as these have no effects on future generations and maintains the separation of species.

In the case of Baby Fae (1984) a heart was transplanted from a healthy baboon to replace Baby Fae's diseased heart. Baby Fae lived

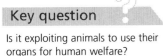

Key question

Is it exploiting animals to use their organs for human welfare?

for three weeks before dying. Many criticised the procedure because it treated the baby as the object of an experiment. But for Peter Singer, who has championed the rights of animals, the critics hypocritically failed to ask two of the most important questions:

> *The traditional sanctity of life ethic forbids us to kill and take the organs of a human being who is not, and never can be, even minimally conscious; and it maintains this refusal even when the parents of the infant favour the donation of organs. At the same time, this ethic accepts without question that we may rear baboons and chimpanzees in order to kill them and use their organs. Why does our ethic draw so sharp a distinction between human beings and all other animals? Why does species membership make such a difference to the ethics of how we may treat a being?*
>
> (Peter Singer, *Rethinking Life and Death*, page 165)

Key people

Andrew Linzey holds the First Fellowship in animal welfare at Oxford University.

But Singer is not entirely right in condemning all those who hold a sanctity of life position that it necessarily leads to the view that animals may be exploited for human benefit. **Andrew Linzey**, for example, has championed a theological animal liberation. Linzey argues that under the influence of Aristotle and Aquinas slavery was justified because not all human beings enjoyed the same degree of rationality (this included women and children). Aquinas used Aristotle's natural law 'belonging to and existing for' distinction to argue that it is not wrong to use something for which it is designed to be. Men are to rule women because women are designed to have children; humans are to rule animals because they are designed to supply human needs. But early on many Christians questioned this Aristotelian distinction; slavery was considered to give too much power to humans and to question God's place as the ultimate authority. It has taken a long time for this strand in Christian teaching to become part of mainstream thinking. Linzey argues that just as slavery in the nineteenth century was abolished and then, later, women given equality with men, so animals today should also become part of the moral community.

Linzey concludes that genetic engineering using animals and organ xenotransplantation should be condemned by Christians as forms of slavery for the simple reason that the 'belonging to and existing for' should not be predicated on humans but God:

Key quote

The human patenting of animals is nothing less than idolatrous.

ANDREW LINZEY

> *No human being can be justified in claiming absolute ownership of animals for the simple reason that God alone owns creation. Animals do not simply exist for us nor belong to us. They exist primarily for God and belong to God. The human patenting of animals is nothing less than idolatrous.*
>
> (Andrew Linzey, *Animal Theology*, page 149)

Presumably if the dead donor rule applies to humans, then it must equally apply to animals as well.

Summary diagram

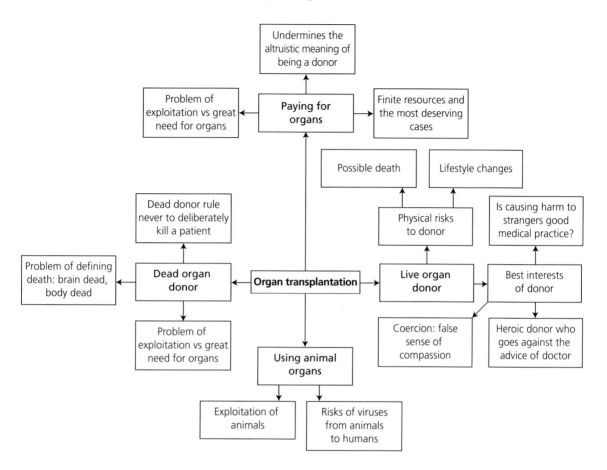

8 Normative ethical responses to organ transplantation

Many of the ethical considerations have been discussed so far; however, the following focuses on some of the key issues raised by different normative ethical systems.

a) Consequentialism
i) Act utilitarianism

An important aspect of the utilitarian ethic is that it questions traditional moral objections by asking whether they have any rational basis to them. For the classical utilitarian who measures whether something is good by the amount of happiness it creates, the fact that I may have a strong moral objection to something is not sufficient reason for stopping someone else from doing it. In many of the considerations above the main arguments have been very simple: if an organ transplantation creates more happiness than pain, when all the risks are considered, then all other objections should be disregarded – even though it may cause moral outrage.

The utilitarians also question whether altruism is a necessary consideration of donorship. This is a difficult area. J.S. Mill acknowledged that action not character (or motive) determines whether an action is good:

> *They are also aware that a right action does not necessarily indicate a virtuous character, and that actions which are blamable, often proceed from qualities entitled to praise…in the long run the best proof of good character is good actions.*
>
> (John Stuart Mill, *Utilitarianism* (edited by Mary Warnock), pages 271–272)

Key quote

Mill on altruism or sacrifice: *'He may be an inspiring proof of what men can do, but assuredly not an example of what they should.'*

UTILITARIANISM, PAGE 267

In other words, although a member of the family may be motivated to act altruistically to give an organ to a relative, his altruism doesn't make the action any better or worse. Utilitarians reject objections to commercial organ transplantation as being irrational. The only consideration is not motivation but whether it causes harm. Furthermore, it might make it easier for the patient to know that the donor has not had to make an unreasonable sacrifice because they have been paid. This might release them from the 'tyranny of the gift' (see page 117). Nevertheless, the loss of gift motivation might be regarded by many as a **slippery slope** to less scrupulous behaviour simply because of the great pressure to provide more organs for transplantation. Presumed consent might be included as an example of a slippery slope where the state controls our bodies in violation of our actual intentions.

ii) Welfare utilitarianism

The welfare utilitarian's main consideration is to deal with qualities that can be demonstrated to enhance the whole of society. The welfare utilitarian therefore might consider that, in the case of the heroic donor, the refusal to take his organ is justified because the medical evidence demonstrates that it will do no one any good. This may appear to place less emphasis on autonomy than many would like, but the welfare utilitarian may consider that autonomy is too abstract a notion and that we do not necessarily act in our own or other people's best interests.

More problematic for welfare utilitarians is how one should **distribute resources**. Tony Hope (see pages 11–12 above) makes a good case for abandoning the **rule of rescue**, however painful this might be, if on finite resources it makes more sense to treat a greater number of patients to increase their average welfare, than to spend a lot of money on expensive treatment for only a few. A doctor has a duty to all his patients, and sometimes he will have to make a difficult decision that some treatments simply cannot be justified. However, this appears to contradict the important medical notion that a doctor will never deliberately harm his patients and that the rule of rescue is justified simply because it would be wrong to deliberately allow an innocent person to die.

b) Natural law

The natural law tradition distinguishes between interior and exterior acts. In the Roman Catholic natural law tradition the teaching of the Church states that, although the 'spontaneous' and generous act of giving an organ, as an interior act, is to be praised, there is no exterior duty to give. It is therefore illicit and intrinsically wrong to take an organ from anyone without their free and rational **consent**. The interior act of a doctor advising and performing an organ transplant must always be one which holds respect for life (the donor and recipient) as paramount; all other intentions will necessarily lead to exploitation.

- **The principle of totality** states that human bodies must always be treated with the utmost respect as the body is the temple of the soul. Unlike animals, for humans the end or *telos* is resurrection. As Christian teaching does not teach that the body should be intact for resurrection, it does nevertheless suggest that it should be given respect even after death. Pope Pius XII (1876–1958) instructed that any mutilation of the body must be reasonable if it is to remove a diseased organ and therefore to preserve the totality of the body. The Church has since developed the principle of totality to allow for donorship of organs if the act of giving preserves the integrity of the spiritual self. This means avoiding putting pressure on donors to give organs unless all the alternatives have first been explored. However, not all Catholic theologians have interpreted the doctrine this way and have rejected all organ transplantations as an infringement of the principle of totality.
- **Live donors.** The Church praises those who act in 'solidarity with others' for the flourishing of society (a primary natural law precept). Live donors who, out of a sense of charity and generosity, give an organ to help someone else earn our highest praise. However, it is wrong to take any organ which *directly* causes long-term harm to the donor and the 'risks incurred by the donor are proportionate to the good sought for the recipient' (*Catechism of the Catholic Church*, paragraph 2296). Only paired organs, or organ parts (such as a liver lobe) which can repair themselves (as in blood donation), may be given.
- **Dead donors.** After a person's death other whole organs may be donated. However, it is intrinsically wrong to take organs from a person before they are completely dead (i.e. in a PVS state) nor is

Key question

Is giving an organ from a live donor to another person breaking natural law?

Key thought

The principle of totality considers that the whole of the human person (body and soul) must be treated with absolute respect.

Key quote

Over and above such outstanding moments, there is an everyday heroism, made up of gestures of sharing, big or small, which builds up an authentic culture of life. A particularly praiseworthy example of such gestures is the donation of organs, performed in an ethically acceptable manner, with a view to offering a chance of health and even of life itself to the sick who sometimes have no other hope.

POPE JOHN PAUL II, *EVANGELIUM VITAE* (1995), PARAGRAPH 86

it permitted to prolong a life so that organs may be taken. All forms of euthanasia are illicit. The Church accepts that death may be defined as 'brain death' but that it must be complete and irreversible. The Church states that 'The free gift of organs after death is legitimate and can be meritorious' (*Catechism of the Catholic Church*, paragraph 2301).

- **Use of animals.** As the *telos* of animals does not include the resurrection because as 'simple things' they lack a rational soul, some of their organs (excluding hearts and reproductive organs) may be used for human transplants.

c) Virtue ethics

Key question

Which virtues does a doctor need when giving advice about organ transplantation?

As we have seen, natural law ethicists have already explored the place of interior acts in relationship to fulfilling one's duty, but this has been almost entirely from the perspective of the donor. However, the virtues may help the doctor or physician in developing the internal goods (attitudes and values) which guide his skills when attempting to judge what is in the best interests of donor and patient. In Aristotelian terms the skill of *phronesis* or prudence is to strike the middle path between the extremes of excess and deficiency, such as promising too much and being too cautious.

- **Performative virtues.** The virtue of honesty is needed for a doctor to inform a patient that he or she will need an organ transplant, but also the finer skills of timing, tone of voice, when to be direct, firm and so on. These 'internal goods' might equally be applied to a possible donor whose offer is not suitable. Virtues are 'value adding' and an integral aspect to the welfare practice of patient and donor; the doctor is not merely a technician but essential to the very process of treatment.
- **Principle-orientated virtues.** Many argue that virtues act to correspond with existing principles to enable them to be practised as humanely as possible. For example, in the question of judging the best interests of the patient and donor when considering alternative treatments, risks involved and availability of resources, the virtues might function by ensuring that the doctor applies the principles fairly, with an open mind, without playing the professional (vice of excess) or on the other hand being too understanding or too empathetic (vices of deficiency).

In virtue ethics donor and doctor are bound together in a common desire to act selflessly and for the good of another. Such an endeavour has more to it than merely treating the patient but is a contribution to the greater flourishing of society. On the other hand, knowing which virtues are appropriate is often very difficult to determine.

d) Kantian ethics

Key question

How can we tell whether a donor's sense of duty is genuine?

In the first instance the Kantian categorical might act as a good means to test whether the consideration of giving an organ for transplantation is a genuine duty. Although generosity cannot be a duty as such, the universalising principle can question whether the act of giving an organ is an autonomous and rational act and not false duties which are in fact emotional such as psychological pressures from others, a sense of heroism or need (for money). What makes these false or merely **hypothetical imperatives** is a lack of authenticity. Kant gives the example of a shopkeeper returning the right change to a customer. Giving the correct change because he feels that it is good for business lacks the authentic good will unlike the giving of the right change because it is always the right thing to do. In the kingdom of ends it could therefore be imagined that citizens who selflessly act for the good of others by giving their organs have achieved the very highest end. In fact the 'stranger as donor' is a model of how we would like everyone to treat each other.

Kantian ethicists are particularly critical of selling organs to recipients because they feel that this cheapens society. If each organ is part of a person and according to the practical imperative it is always wrong to use a person as a means to an end, then the **commodification** of body parts fails to respect the donor and, by extension, others in society.

But the weakness of the Kantian argument is that organs are seen in some way to take on lives of their own and to become persons. But if it was my car I was offering to give to a person in need it might be appropriate to give it away for nothing or for a low price. No one is going to criticise me for thinking economically or even emotionally about selling or giving away an object. In the same way a kidney is not a person; selling it does not cheapen society and in the competitive market place it may mean that some people gain more for their product than others. If an organ is an object, then the Kantian way of thinking may have very little to say about organ transplantation from live donors, except that the act must be autonomous and voluntary.

Key word

Commodification means to treat the body as an object which can be bought and sold.

e) Revealed ethics

Whereas many of the arguments so far have given a high priority to the autonomy of the individual to decide on how his body is to be used, revealed ethics begins with the principle of 'disfiguring the dead'. Biblical law forbids leaving an executed person's body overnight and stipulates that it should be buried the same day (Deuteronomy 21:22–23). In the Jewish tradition this was taken to mean that all human bodies should be buried as soon as possible. All

bodies are therefore seen as representing the divine image (Genesis
1:27); respect for all bodies, whether alive or dead, is not so much
out of respect for the person themselves but for God.

However, respect for dead bodies has to be balanced against the
Biblical law to save lives. However, the right to break one law with
another may only happen when it can be shown that it was
necessary and that other courses of action have been considered. In
Judaism the law to save life takes precedence over all other laws
(except the laws against bloodshed, idolatry and incest) but the
question is whether disfiguring a body to take an organ is
necessarily a life-saving action. For example, an autopsy (an
investigation of a body after death to find out the causes of death) is
not directly saving a life, and a kidney donation may improve the
quality of someone's life even if their condition is not life-
threatening. Both cases may justify disfigurement because in the first
case it is contributing to medical knowledge to save future lives and
in the second case saving a life means enabling a person to live life
more fully.

For Christians the view of the body is shaped by two notions:
the incarnation and the resurrection. The incarnation (God
becoming human in Jesus Christ) reaffirms the body as something
sacred to be treated with respect as a psycho-physical whole. But
Christians are called on to be generous and sacrificial in their
treatment of their neighbours. The New Testament offers particular
insights into the use of the body for others:

- **Respect for the body**. Respect for our bodies is due to the fact
  that they are animated by God's Spirit. In the Old Testament God
  breathes his Spirit into Adam (Genesis 2:7) to indicate that
  human life is intimately related to God. It is for this reason that
  Paul writes that we have a duty to respect all parts of our bodies:
  'The immoral man sins against his own body. Do you not know
  that your body is a temple of the Holy Spirit within you which
  you have from God?' (1 Corinthians 6:18–19).
- **Generosity and healing**. Jesus commands his own disciples 'Heal
  the sick, raise the dead, cleanse lepers, cast out demons. You
  received without pay, give without pay' (Matthew 10:8). Giving
  organs to aid the sick can therefore be seen as a supremely
  sacrificial act in loving one's neighbour (Mark 12:31). Payment
  for organs is clearly forbidden.
- **Resurrection**. In the final resurrected state the earthly body is
  transformed (1 Corinthians 15:51–53) so that there is no need
  for the physical body at death. This suggests, as we have seen, that
  providing the body is treated with respect then organs may be
  donated for research or for transplantation.

However, there are Christian minorities who argue that organ transplantation is wrong. Christian Scientists believe, for example, that the spirit–body relationship enables the spirit to heal the body and that the deliberate removal of organs destroys body–spirit integrity.

On the other hand, there are the **radical liberals** such as Joseph Fletcher who argue that it makes no sense to dispose of a body when its organs can be used to help others. The objections raised by various Christian traditions often do so based on outmoded and irrational taboos about the body. Christian love should encourage all people to donate their bodies for the use of others, so that they might live full and happy lives.

Key quote

The day is coming, we may hope, when memorial services will take the place of selfish and unethical religious burial ceremonies.

JOSEPH FLETCHER, *HUMANHOOD*, PAGE 78

Study guide

By the end of this chapter, you should have considered the advantages and disadvantages of giving and receiving an organ for transplantation and the debate about consent and presumed consent. You should also have assessed the problems of defining death when acquiring organs from dead donors and the medical ethical dilemma of causing harm to live donors. You should have also considered the various normative ethical systems in relation to these issues as well as the proposal that when organs are in short supply they could be paid for or taken from animals.

Revision checklist

Can you explain:

- the dead donor rule
- the problem of defining death
- the problem of defining consent
- the problems for the patient receiving a donor organ
- the risks involved being a donor
- why taking an organ from a live donor poses medical ethical issues.

Can you apply:

- welfare utilitarianism to consideration of the rule of rescue and distribution of resources
- Kantian ethics to authentic donorship and the commodification of organs
- virtue ethics to the doctor's role in treatment of donor and patient.

Can you give arguments for and against:

- xenotransplantation
- commercial buying and selling of human organs
- heroic donors and strangers as donors.

Essay question

1. 'The best use of dead bodies is to presume that their organs can be taken to help those who are living but need replacement organs.' Discuss.

The essay might begin by explaining what consent is and why it is valued in most moral systems. A survey of the value of consent from Kant in terms of rationality and autonomy, Mill in terms of harm and revealed Christian ethics in terms of human dignity might help to establish the view that consent is crucial in most discussions about organ transplantations. The essay might then consider the status of the dead body in terms of rights and the dead donor rule. The case for presumed consent can then be put forward in simple terms as a means of resolving the major shortage of organs.

The evaluative element of the essay should include the argument against presumed consent. For instance, it gives the state too much power and symbolically undermines the autonomy of individuals even though they may have no need of their bodies, and it distorts the value of donorship as a free and generous act. Other forms of acquiring organs might be considered preferable (commercial or animals). On the other hand to refuse presumed consent might be considered selfish; we should ignore altruism and concentrate on making the living happy. These views might be reviewed from at least one normative ethical system.

Further essay questions

2a   Explain what is meant by a quality of life argument.

2b   'There is nothing wrong paying for an organ from a healthy person to help a sick person.' Discuss.

3a   Explain how welfare utilitarians approach the issue of organ transplantation.

3b   Assess the view that it is a better use of medical resources to help ten fairly ill people than one very sick person.

4   Discuss the moral problems caused by the use of animal organs to replace defective human organs.

Chapter checklist

The first part of the chapter looks at the reasons for and processes of human cloning. The distinction between therapeutic and reproductive cloning is considered as well as the risks involved. Reproductive cloning is reviewed by considering whether it devalues human dignity and in the context of theories about free will and determinism. The use of animal eggs in cloning of humans is discussed. Various normative ethical responses to cloning are surveyed.

1 Why clone?

Cloning offers another biotechnology with possible alternatives to cure diseases and help overcome reproductive problems. For example, in the case of Dr Shann (see pages 114–115 above), cloning could offer him one or more solutions to the dilemma he faced with the two babies:

● he could have cloned both babies to replace them
● he could have cloned Baby A to replace or repair his damaged heart.

Cloning has been used for some time for reproducing specialised crops but since **Dolly the Sheep**, the first mammal to be produced through cloning in 1997, cloning also offers farmers the prospect of cloning prize animals and avoiding the haphazard breeding of animals through normal sexual reproduction. However, although there has been some success in cloning plants and animals (and in 2007 the cloning of an adult monkey embryo), cloning human beings has been much more problematic. Extravagant claims have been made about the success of human cloning but in reality the science is still in its very early days. The possibilities open to Dr Shann are not nearly as optimistic as they might first appear.

Skin cells taken from Semos the adult macaque were cloned to create an embryo from which stem cells were extracted. This marks a major breakthrough in primate cloning and suggests that it might be possible for humans also to be cloned.

a) Types of cloning

The term 'clone' is from the Greek meaning a 'branch' or a 'cutting from a branch'. However, cloning covers a range of processes found in nature.

- **Asexual reproduction.** Nicholas Agar, for example, defines a clone as 'an organism whose beginning is not marked by a sexual event' (*Perfect Copy*, page 21). This happens in nature at the lower end of biological sophistication when an organism naturally divides itself (e.g. dandelions and aphids) and its offspring therefore is an exact copy with the same **genome**. A 'sexual event' by contrast requires two organisms to pass on their joint DNA (i.e. 23 chromosomes from each human parent) through physical union to produce offspring. Asexual cloning, on the other hand, requires no combining of DNA and the offspring of the parent therefore share exactly the same genome.
- **Mitosis** is when cells divide, producing identical copies of themselves. This occurs all the time in organisms in the production of new cells.
- **Monozygotic twins** can occur naturally when the zygote splits and becomes two or more offspring, all having the same set of chromosomes. This can happen asymmetrically where the first embryo produces a new embryo or symmetrically where the original embryo is destroyed, producing two new embryos (both having the same set of chromosomes). This is sometimes referred to as embryo splitting.

There is no consensus among biologists why sexual reproduction has evolved. Some suggest that this process reduces the chances of a whole species being wiped out by a virus by adding variety to the gene pool. Others suggest that sex helps higher animals to develop their social skills and sophisticated relationships.

b) Two ways of creating a clone

However, in the cloning debate, cloning is often an emotive term because the process of creating a replica offspring requires a deliberate process of interference. There are two ways of creating a clone:

1 **Cell nuclear replacement (CNR)** or **somatic cell nuclear transfer (SCNT)**. Both methods involve 'enucleating' or removing the nucleus from an unfertilised ovum (egg) and replacing it with the nucleus from an adult (or developed embryo or foetus) somatic human cell. A small electric shock or chemical is given to the cell which prompts it to divide. The cells are genetically almost an exact copy of the adult. However, the ovum contains **mitochondria** which have their own DNA. The

mitochondria cause slight differences between the clone and the cell donor (unless the cell donor and the egg donor come from the same person). This means that although the clone will be almost identical to the adult it will not be exactly the same.

2 **Embryonic splitting** (or 'biopsy'). Genetically identical individuals are created by dividing embryo cells usually at the 8-cell stage and before the primitive streak stage at 14 days. This has been used for producing cattle and mimics the way in which monozygotic twins are produced. It has a high mortality rate when applied to human embryos.

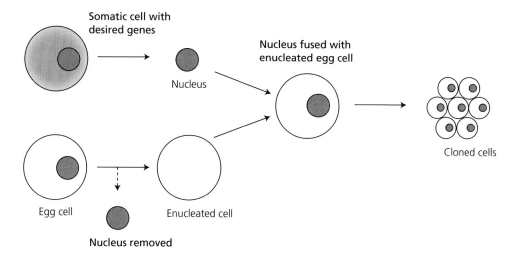

Somatic cell with desired genes

Nucleus fused with enucleated egg cell

Nucleus

Cloned cells

Egg cell

Enucleated cell

Nucleus removed

Somatic cell nuclear transfer.

Key question

What is the purpose of therapeutic and reproductive cloning?

c) Therapeutic and reproductive cloning

It has become usual to refer to two kinds of cloning: reproductive and therapeutic. The terms are often considered to be confusing as there is no biological difference between the two; the difference lies in their aims:

● **Reproductive cloning.** The aim of this form of cloning occurs when CNR or SCNT has occurred through IVF and then the embryo is placed into a surrogate woman's womb. The intention, therefore, is for the cloned embryo to develop into a fully grown human being. A human clone would provide exact matches for blood transfusions, cancer treatment, kidney failure and so on for the adult donor from whom the somatic cell was taken. Or it could be seen as another form of assisted reproduction for parents who are unable to have children using other methods but want a child genetically related to one of them or to replace a lost child (as in the Dr Shann case on pages 114–115 above).

● **Therapeutic cloning.** The aim of this form of cloning is to produce **embryonic stem cells** which will be an exact match for the donor from whom the somatic cell was taken. The stem cells can be induced to form particular human organs or tissues to replace damaged or diseased organs and tissues in the donor. The advantage with cloning stem cells is that they won't be rejected by the donor body and therefore there will be no need for powerful and expensive anti-rejection drugs.

Cross-reference

Read pages 104–105 above to find out how embryonic stem cells are obtained.

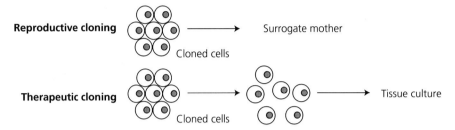

The two aims of cloning: therapeutic and reproductive.

Both terms are problematic. Some people dislike the term therapeutic cloning because although it may offer aid to the donor the process destroys the pre-embryo which cannot be good for it. Others dislike the term because it masks the fact that all human cloning is reproductive, and for some the pre-embryo is a life and entitled to the same rights and protection as any other human life.

2 The law and human cloning

The **Human Fertilisation and Embryology Bill** (2008) will incorporate the Human Reproductive Act (2001) and make it an offence to 'place in a woman a human embryo which has been created otherwise than by fertilisation' – that is, human eggs and sperm 'whose nuclear or mitochondrial DNA has not been altered'. An embryo may be placed in a woman's womb if 'no cell has been added to it other than by division of the embryo's own cells' (paragraph 3). Effectively this allows therapeutic cloning and embryo research but rejects reproductive cloning.

However, there are arguments for the use of animal gametes, especially ova (eggs), because of the shortage of human eggs. The creation of cloned **chimeras** and **hybrids** using SCNT or CNR is permitted by the Bill. These are referred to in the Bill as 'inter-species embryos'. The aim is to allow research: to test the capacity of embryonic stem cells to differentiate into a range of body cell types; as part of research into the treatment of serious diseases; and to derive human embryonic stem cells, so as to avoid the shortage of good quality human eggs available for research.

Key words

A **chimera** is an organism containing a mixture of different genetic tissues which originated from different zygotes or the fusing together of early embryos.

A **hybrid** is created by cross-breeding different animals.

The law also states the following concerning the use of inter-species embryos:

- *A human embryo cannot be placed in an animal, or an animal embryo in a human being.*
- *Only a human embryo, or human gametes, may be placed in a woman.*
- *Human and animal gametes cannot be mixed except for research purposes and under licence to test human sperm.*
- *The result of the mixed gametes must be destroyed when the test is complete.*
- *Their creation is legal for research purposes provided they are destroyed before the primitive streak or by 14 days.*
- *It is illegal to implant an inter-species embryo in a woman.*
  (based on *The Human Embryology and Fertilisation Bill* (2008), paragraph 4)

3 Risks of cloning

Reproductive human cloning (placing the clone in the woman's womb) is illegal in 35 countries throughout the world.

a) Results of animal cloning

However, even supposing it could work, the results of animal reproductive cloning indicate the following risks which could equally be human risks:

- **Very low level of success.** In the case of Dolly the Sheep, from 227 enucleated ova, 29 embryos were produced, of which only one, Dolly, developed into a live birth. Since then the process has become more efficient from 0.4 per cent (Dolly) to 6 per cent success, but this compares very poorly with the 20–40 per cent success rate of IVF. This makes reproductive cloning very expensive both in cash terms and in the number of eggs needed to carry out SCNT.
- **'Large off-spring syndrome'.** Many cloned foetuses (e.g. sheep/cows) are a third larger than normal with swollen internal organs, which can kill or badly damage the surrogate mother.
- **Other ailments.** At the moment animal clones suffer from mental deficiencies, respiratory failures and early arthritis.
- **Premature ageing.** The use of adult cells for the nucleus transfer appears to set a biological time much older than the age of the cloned animal even though the somatic adult cell has, in theory, been switched off. Premature ageing therefore brings with it the problems associated with old age.

● **Germ line problems**. It is impossible to know whether the defects in the clone will be passed on to the next generation or in what ways the gene pool might become weakened.

There are fears also that reproductive cloning for animals as well as humans will reduce the natural variety found through sexual reproduction. But this would only be true if cloning were to be carried out on a large scale. As with all scientific endeavours some of the problems listed above will in all likelihood be overcome, but the question is whether the risks are worth it.

b) Therapeutic human cloning

The risks of therapeutic cloning for humans might include:

● **Exaggerated claims**. In 2001 the **Advanced Cell Technology** company in the USA cloned the first embryonic stem cells. They had previously had some success using cloned embryonic stem cells in a mouse's damaged spinal cord. However, cloned human embryos at present rarely live more than a few days. Even persuading cells to become tissues is a complex task, let alone constructing all the various cell parts to become an organ. The furthest that scientists have got is the creation of rudimentary liver and some tissue cells. Claims to have found wonder cures are misleading and set up false expectations of what can be done.
● **Egg donors**. The process of donating eggs is painful and potentially dangerous. Eggs do not freeze easily and so need to be used quickly. Those cloned embryos which are not used have then to be disposed of. The use of animal eggs is limited by legislation to experimental use. Therapeutic cloning will, therefore, be limited by the supply of eggs or to the use of aborted foetus eggs.
● **Embryonic stem cells**. The creation of embryonic stem cells involves the destruction of the cloned embryo. This inevitably raises problems with the status of the early embryo. Even embryonic stem cells (ES) may not behave as predicted and cells can mutate and form cancers or tumours because once transplanted the stem cells appear to revert back to their adult cell state. Some tumours have been found to be made up of bone and hair cells.

Cross-reference

Read pages 91–93 on the problems with the status of the early embryo.

4 Nature, human nature and free will

Key question

Even if cloning is playing God should it necessarily be forbidden?

Cloning (especially reproductive cloning) more than any other form of genetic engineering has challenged us to consider who we are and what our place is in nature. For some the new cloning technology offers an optimistic hope that we can take control and exploit the potentials of nature for ourselves. But for others, the fear

Key quote

We used to think our fate was in our stars. Now we know that in large measure our fate is in our genes.

JAMES WATSON, ON COMPLETION OF THE
HUMAN GENOME PROJECT

is that cloning of whatever kind will alienate us from nature and make us view it and ourselves far too mechanistically.

There is no consensus among religious and non-religious thinkers whether cloning is to be rejected or accepted. Many theologians, for example, consider that what makes us human is our ability to use our talents to develop ourselves and the world in new and exciting ways. They embrace what science offers. On the other hand some secular thinkers worry that cloning technology will convince us that we have no significant moral role to play as it will diminish our sense of free will and moral responsibility.

a) Pessimism and the genomic trap

Key thought

The human genome is the complete list of coded instructions (DNA) needed to make a person. The Human Genome Project was the largest international collaboration between scientists ever undertaken. Between 1990 and 2003, thousands of scientists worldwide undertook the immense task of sequencing the 3 billion bases of genetic information that resides in every human cell (http://genome.wellcome.ac.uk).

Rosemary Tong is one example of a secular philosopher who fears that cloning will only add to the tendency to dehumanise ourselves and present the human merely as a complex mechanical object. She argues that **The Human Genome Project** has challenged our understanding of ourselves, our nature and connections with our ancestors and descendants. Genetics has undermined our sense of freedom, because it challenges the notion that we determine who we are. She argues that 'The Human Genome Project will only increase our tendency to explain all our physical and psychological diseases, defects and disorders as a simple product of our genetic structure' (*Feminist Approaches to Bioethics*, page 230). We have a moral duty to ensure that we do not fall into the **genomic trap** whereby we solve all our problems by eliminating people who might be diseased or a problem to a society.

b) Optimism and liberation

There are some, such as the visionary biologist and theologian **Pierre Teilhard de Chardin** (1881–1955), who argue that genetic control as a means of eugenics will allow us to 'seize the tiller' and direct evolution to what de Chardin called 'the omega point', the stage where humans are truly free and no longer dependent on nature.

Key people

Ian Barbour is Bean Professor Emeritus of Science, Technology and Society at Carleton College, Minnesota, USA. He is one of the most influential theologians today in the area of science and religion.

Ian Barbour, on the other hand, takes a more cautious but positive view of our use of technology. As a **process theologian** he believes that nature is not static but dynamic and open-ended with endless possibilities. As human beings we have the unique intelligence to develop nature creatively in many new and exciting ways. Cloning is just one technology which with care could be used to enhance our existence. This is why he rejects the view that we should not play God with nature:

> *Other critics claim that we are 'playing God' and usurping the divine prerogatives when we try and modify human genes. I would reply that creation was not completed once-for-all. I have suggested that God works through the continuing evolutionary process and through our lives today.*

Human beings are endowed with intelligence and creativity. We can be coworkers with God in the fulfilment of God's purposes. As coworkers we can cooperate with God in the continuing creation in nature and history.

(Ian Barbour, *Nature, Human Nature and God*, page 70)

c) Repugnancy and human dignity

One of the most influential writers in this area is **Leon Kass**. Kass argues that we have a set of intuitions that certain things are wrong because they go against nature and human dignity. As with all intuitional theories the problem is that it is very hard to prove an intuition or use one rationally to demonstrate why something is right or wrong. But Kass suggests that from our reactions of horror to certain situations there is 'wisdom of repugnancy'. What he means is that we can, with reflection and reason, work from these reactions to enquire what it is that deep down we find offensive. For example human cloning appears to undermine human dignity; it breaks down the purpose of sex and human complementary relationships between men and women. Here is how he put it in a lecture given to the President's Council on Bioethics:

It is difficult to put this disquiet into words. We are in an area where initial repugnancies are hard to translate into sound moral arguments. We are probably repelled by the idea of drugs that erase memories or that change personalities, or at interventions that enable seventy-year-olds to bear children or play professional sports, or, to engage in some wilder imaginings, of mechanical implants that enable men to nurse infants or computer-body hookups that would enable us to download the OED [The Oxford English Dictionary]. But is there wisdom in this repugnance? Taken one person at a time, with a properly prepared set of conditions and qualifications, it is going to be hard to say what is wrong with any biotechnical intervention that could give us (more) ageless bodies or make it possible for us to have happier souls. If there is a case to be made against these activities – for individuals – we sense that it may have something to do with what is natural, or what is humanly dignified, or what is the attitude that is properly respectful of what is naturally and dignifiedly human.

(Leon R. Kass, *Beyond Therapy: Biotechnology and the Pursuit of Human Improvement*, lecture given to the President's Council on Bioethics, 2003, www.bioethics.gov/background/kasspaper.html)

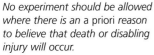
Kass' argument supports the **Nuremberg Code** (1947) which specifically forbids experimentation on human beings. This would appear to reject therapeutic cloning for those who regard the early embryo as a human being but it would also disallow reproductive cloning because of the risks involved and the intuition that it would create a second-class person whose purpose would be for scientists to see whether the cloning experiment could work.

Key question

If reproductive cloning of humans were possible, would the clone lack a soul or free will?

Key word

Ontological means the discussion or description of how something actually exists.

d) Reproductive cloning: identity and free will

Supposing reproductive cloning was to be achieved, what might this indicate about human free will and moral responsibility?

The first question is whether a cloned human being would be any less a person than a human conceived sexually. On almost every account there would be no **ontological** reason to suppose that a clone would be different from any other human being.

From a scientific point of view a cloned human would still have a complete set of 46 chromosomes, and even if these chromosomes were the same as the donor, this would be no different from that of monozygotic twins (and we presume that both are separate persons). In fact cloned humans may be genetically more different from monozygotic twins because of the mitochondrial DNA acquired from the ovum.

From a theological perspective the soul or animating principle operates through the physical body from the moment it emerges as an individual human being (when this occurs, as we have seen, is a matter of dispute).

But for scientists and theologians what makes any human an individual personality is a combination of our genes (we each have around 30,000 genes), environment, hormones and experience. Our personality is an 'emergent property'; it is not predetermined but results from the complex relationship of all these factors. It may be that a particular gene has a very great effect on the whole body and fundamentally affects the person, such as the gene for cystic fibrosis or Huntington's disease. But in general genes set up potentials and predispositions; they do not in themselves create persons.

Nevertheless, even though there may be no ontological problem with a cloned human being considered a person, there may be powerful psychological objections.

- The cloned person might feel that they lack the usual life story which everyone else has beginning with a sexual act of two people, who themselves are the product of a long line of relationships.
- The cloned person might feel inferior to his or her donor who represents the real person whereas they are merely a copy.
- A clone might be regarded as a deficient human (as a form of racism) because their function is only to provide tissue or organs.

Finally, cloning could have the effect of blunting our sense of moral responsibility. If humans can be created asexually, then it appears to remove that special quality called 'free will'. Leon Kass has been one of the more vocal opponents to genetic enhancement because he feels that it reduces the element of chance which makes human lives rich and interesting. But this is only true if we believe there is something called free will.

Cross-references

Read pages 98–101 above on gene therapy and enhancement.

For a more detailed analysis of free will and determinism read Mel Thompson, *Ethical Theory*, Chapter 3.

- **Hard determinists**. Reproductive cloning makes no difference to those who consider that free will is an illusion. Although hard determinists consider that we have desires and we will certain things to happen, ultimately our actions are the result of so many factors outside our control that we cannot be held ultimately responsible for what we do. Determinists of this kind are reductionists because they believe everything can be explained in physical terms. The hard determinist might even support cloning and gene therapy because it would be better to remove dangerous people from society than allow nature to take its course.
- **Soft determinists**. Soft determinists are compatibilists because they believe humans have free will which can select and change events, but it is not a special 'causal power' which is totally independent from other causes in the world. We are affected by our genes but we can overcome our predispositions to some extent. For example I may be naturally greedy but I can choose not to have a second helping of pudding. The soft determinist therefore warns that the balance between free will and genes is complex. Gene therapy and cloning could so alter a person's biological make-up that their free will becomes ineffective.
- **Libertarians**. Libertarians, such as Kant, argued for an independent special inner (or 'noumenal') causal power called the 'free-will'. The free-will operates within the physical constraints of the world but ultimately decides what action is to be taken. Kant's free will suggests that we have enormous responsibility not to exercise the free-will in any way that diminishes us. Cloning, therefore, is not a threat to the libertarian. But the libertarian would criticise the cloned human being who used his asexual origins as an excuse not to behave morally.

5 The use of animals: chimeras and hybrids

Key question

Is there anything intrinsically wrong in the creation of human–animal hybrids for medical research?

The creation of hybrids is not new. A mule is a cross between a female horse and a male donkey and in 1984 scientists created the first sheep–goat chimera, the 'geep'. But animal–human cloning is new and controversial; President Bush's State of the Union address in 2006 specifically cited human–animal hybrids as an example of the gross misuse of medical research.

A hopeful society has institutions of science and medicine that do not cut ethical corners, and that recognize the matchless value of every life. Tonight I ask you to pass legislation to prohibit the most egregious abuses of medical research: human cloning in all its forms, creating or implanting embryos for experiments, creating human–animal hybrids,

Key quote

Human life is a gift from our Creator – and that gift should never be discarded, devalued or put up for sale.

GEORGE W. BUSH

and buying, selling, or patenting human embryos. Human life is a gift from our Creator – and that gift should never be discarded, devalued or put up for sale.

(President George W. Bush, State of the Union address, January 2006, www.whitehouse.gov/stateoftheunion/2006)

The reasons for wanting to create animal–human embryos (or 'cybrids' as they have been nicknamed) is because of the great shortage and expense of using human ova (eggs) – about £3000 for each woman. It would allow scientists to use animal eggs with human adult cells to carry out their experiments much more cheaply. Cow eggs were first used in 1991 and rabbit hybrids in 2003. Both were used to create stem cells to help scientists in their research on embryonic stem cells (ES). However, hybrid stem cells cannot at the moment be used directly for treatments because the mitochondria DNA from the animal might be attacked by the human immune system.

A major argument against hybrids is that it breaks the **species barrier**. However, defining this barrier is not easy. The human genome contains many genes whose proteins are necessary to keep cells alive and growing. But these genes are found in many other organisms where the differences from human genes are only very slight. In addition the human genome has many genes which appear to have no function – one set of genes, for example, is the same as a mouse tail. So, rejection on grounds that animals are very different from humans, and that the species barrier should not be broken, is not as clear cut as it at first seems.

However, some argue that as the genetic argument against human–animal hybrids fails to be convincing, then we should begin with a metaphysical a priori that humans are uniquely different because of their **special relationship with God**. As humans alone are made in the image of God, then they have a duty to maintain the animal world and not exploit it. This, for example, is the conclusion of the Church of Scotland's response to the proposed Human Fertilisation and Embryology Act:

In the historic Christian tradition (drawing on Hebrew scriptures) humans are believed to be uniquely created in God's image and set apart from all other creatures spiritually and have a unique moral responsibility which animals do not have. While humans are given the task of caring for the animal kingdom as fellow creatures of God, they are not seen as of equal status to humans. Intercourse between animals and humans is also expressly condemned.

(Church of Scotland: Church and Society Council and its Society, Religion and Technology Project, 2005)

6 Normative ethical responses to human cloning

a) Utilitarianism

Utilitarian arguments must be based on what we can know or predict about the future based on scientific knowledge. As we have seen, therapeutic cloning can go very badly wrong because cloned cells can revert back to type or become badly cancerous. On the other hand there are clear advantages once the techniques have developed to offer the opportunity to overcome life-crippling diseases.

Other considerations are the huge expense which all forms of cloning incur and the problems of finding enough donor eggs. Some might question whether the ends justify the means given the extreme **unlikelihood** of a cure for Alzheimer's and other diseases happening for some time. It might be that cloning could never offer the cures which the media frequently suggest it can do.

To summarise some of the arguments covered so far, the utilitarian arguments against reproductive cloning include:

- **Risks**. Concerns must take into account the enormous risks involved. There are no guarantees that a clone will live a happy normal life: it may die early, age more quickly or develop unforeseen disabilities. It may be subject to a psychological sense of inferiority.
- **Identity and eugenics**. The problem of identity can be seen in two ways. Firstly, how will society consider a clone? Will the clone be a person with an independent identity from its original? Secondly, how will the clone perceive itself? Would it consider itself to have an independent identity of its own or think of itself as morally and spiritually inferior to its original? If the latter, then it seems to be getting very close to the grossly immoral forms of ideological eugenics which discriminates against some humans because they are considered to be biologically inferior.
- **Distribution and resources**. Some argue that the money spent on cloning could be better used to benefit many others. Stem cells and gene therapy (see Chapter 7) need not involve cloning or embryonic stem (ES) cells. There is also the fear that those who have a great deal of money will be the only ones who could afford to buy the technology, so that rather than being for the benefit of the many, as the 'greatest happiness of the greatest number', there will only be a few very happy people (presuming that cloning could offer the potential cures without risks).

Cross-reference

Read page 22 above on Kant's practical imperative.

b) Kantian ethics

A standard Kantian response to many forms of medical experimentation is that it uses the human being as a means to an end;

it 'instrumentalises' the person by treating them as a **commodity**. This argument relies in particular on the practical imperative.

However, Kantians might not rule out therapeutic cloning altogether. Using the first formulation of the categorical imperative we could well imagine that all people might wish to live with fewer physical disabilities and to be able to repair damaged tissues or even diseased organs. Therefore a person might consider it his absolute duty to use the potential cures which therapeutic cloning offers.

But, at the same time, it is difficult to see how an embryonic clone would possibly consent to be 'cannibalised' either for stem cells (therapeutic cloning) or an adult for organ parts (reproductive cloning). This is especially true of reproductive cloning and the subject matter of science fiction horror movies such as *Parts: The Clonus Horror* (1979) where human clones are bred for their body parts to replace defective organs of the elite members of society. Although the film is a science fiction fantasy, it illustrates Leon Kass' notion of repugnance, the deep-seated sense that we are disgusted that we could even countenance cloning because of what it might lead to.

Indeed some have worried that all forms of cloning could result in a new form of racism or even speciesism which discriminates against human clones as a subhuman underclass with no rights at all.

- **Rights**. Kant's argument begs the question whether a potential life can have any concrete moral status. Embryonic cloning is only morally significant if a potential life can be attributed with appropriate moral status. For the Kantian to consider the embryo to be a full moral agent, the embryo would have to have some form of rationality and this at the very least could not be the case until the foetus develops brain waves around 54 days.

- **Autonomy and the randomness of procreation**. Kantians might argue that reproductive cloning may also have the effect of existentially dehumanising the cloned person by making them feel that they have no authentic means of making original choices. The cloned person might feel that it is the donor who lives the authentic life, because as **Jean-Paul Sartre** describes it, the donor's **existence precedes his essence**. The donor invents his essence (his personality) through genuine free choices, whereas the clone's personality has been decided by the donor – his essence precedes his existence – at least that is how it may feel to him. This may provide a good reason to support the randomness of sexual procreation, where the genes of the offspring are sufficiently different from the offspring's parents that he or she feels they are free to make their own authentic and independent decisions.

Cross-references

Read pages 87–88 on embryo research above.

For more information about Jean-Paul Sartre's existential ethics read Mel Thompson, *Ethical Theory*, Chapter 12.

Key quote

What do we mean by saying that existence precedes essence? We mean that man first of all exists, encounters himself, surges up in the world – and defines himself afterwards.

JEAN-PAUL SARTRE, *EXISTENTIALISM AND HUMANISM* (1948), PAGE 28

c) Virtue ethics

Virtue ethicists might begin by considering to what extent cloning leads to a flourishing society. This might be done by being wary of the misleading headlines of the press or emotional conservative religious groups and by building an argument on **rational** grounds, asking whether these technologies are selfish and unfair. It might also ask whether the use of therapeutic cloning is the best way of gaining scientific knowledge, or whether it just presents an exciting scientific challenge with no concern for human beneficence. The prospect of fame has already enticed several scientists to claim that they have been able to create a human which has turned out to be false. Such dishonest use of science and technology only confirms the fear that cloning is being pursued for its own sake and not for the flourishing (*eudaimonia*) of society (*polis*).

- **Narrative coherence.** An area of debate developed by Alasdair MacIntyre's virtue ethical theory is the need to have a coherent sense of one's own identity. Would a cloned human lack a sense of a story which begins with the sexual intercourse of two people? Would he or she sense that they are not part of the usual narrative of the family, society, nation to which everyone else belongs? If so, then their value as a person with a genuine sense of belonging might be severely undermined.
- **Power and elitism.** Whereas in the Christian tradition benevolence has been a fundamentally important virtue in willing our neighbour's good and caution against cloning and other techniques as being unsafe, the virtues as developed by **Frederick Nietzsche** (1844–1900) present us with a very different approach. Nietzsche's chief virtue is the 'will to power', that is, the ability to say 'yes' to existence and to embrace it in all its fullness. This 'master morality', as he called it, embraces anything which could be seen to advance human existence and that means recognising that the so-called virtues which preserve and protect the weak are in fact vices. Therefore, we might conclude that Nietzsche's great 'yes' to life supports the enormous potential of cloning, not only for its therapeutic abilities, but for developing adult humans to their full potential. This echoes Aristotle's notion that the exercise of the virtues or excellences (*arete* in Greek, meaning excellence of character) suggests that risk-taking is part of being human in the pursuit of perfection and nobility.

d) Natural law

Some have argued that because cloning occurs in nature with embryo splitting and the production of monozygotic twins, then all

Cross-reference

To find out more about Nietzsche's moral philosophy read Mel Thompson, *Ethical Theory*, Chapter 11.

Key quote

The goal of humanity cannot lie at the end, but only in its highest specimens.

FREDERICK NIETZSCHE, *THE UNTIMELY MEDITATIONS* II. 9 (1873)

Key question

If cloning occurs in nature then is it right for humans to develop cloning?

that scientists are doing is developing this process in a more controlled way. The answer given by most natural ethicists is that because something exists in nature this doesn't mean it is necessarily good or right. Natural law asks what the purpose (or *telos*) of anything is *first* and then what means are needed in order to fulfil that end. As spontaneous asexual cloning in humans is the exception to the usual process of reproduction it would be wrong to draw from this that there is a general moral law of nature that makes it good for us to do so. Artificial human cloning of any kind is intrinsically wrong.

This conclusion can be tested in various other ways according to natural law:

- *Eudaimonia* **and human flourishing.** The purpose or final cause of any action must be to enable humans to realise their potentials in order to flourish and live fulfilled lives. There are many reasons why cloning does not do this. There is some evidence that monozygotic twins suffer higher incidences of psychological stress and are prone to more diseases than those who are not cloned in this way.

- **Sex and openness to life.** The Roman Catholic encyclical *Humanae Vitae* (1968) states the natural law notion that every act of sexual conjugal (married) intercourse must be open to new life. Sex must be unitive (loving) and procreative (creating a new life). This is the purpose and *telos* of sex. As cloning is asexual it destroys the unitive–procreative intention, in what Aquinas calls the efficient cause, and is therefore intrinsically wrong. In addition natural law ethicists stress that cloning and gene therapy remove the randomness of sexual procreation which gives to each individual their own unique *telos*.

- **Ordering of nature and society.** Natural law recognises that the purpose of morality is also to achieve the 'right ordering of society'. Reproductive cloning deliberately confuses family relationships. A woman who is the adult cell donor and provides her enucleated egg for cloning is therefore both mother and sister to her offspring. The relationship between them is confused; one moment the woman is the nurturer, next the sibling. The clear delineation of responsibilities cannot be good for their relationship or the flourishing of society.

In addition to external actions, natural law is achieved through interior law or good intentions. These virtues guide reason to develop our characters so that we choose to do good. Cloning which occurs in nature cannot be bad, but deliberate cloning is selfish and because it causes death (the early embryo has to be destroyed for the ES cells) it commits homicide. The Catholic Church states in the 'Instruction on Respect for Human Life in its

> ## Key quote
>
> *Nonetheless the Church, calling men back to the observance of the norms of the natural law, as interpreted by their constant doctrine, teaches that each and every marriage act must remain open to the transmission of life.*
>
> *HUMANAE VITAE*, PARAGRAPH 11

Origin and on the Dignity of Procreation Replies to Certain Questions of the Day', otherwise known as *Donum Vitae* (1987):

> *Techniques of fertilization* in vitro *can open the way to other forms of biological and genetic manipulation of human embryos, such as attempts or plans for fertilization between human and animal gametes and the gestation of human embryos in the uterus of animals, or the hypothesis or project of constructing artificial uteruses for the human embryo. These procedures are contrary to the human dignity proper to the embryo, and at the same time they are contrary to the right of every person to be conceived and to be born within marriage and from marriage. Also, attempts or hypotheses for obtaining a human being without any connection with sexuality through 'twin fission', cloning or parthenogenesis are to be considered contrary to the moral law, since they are in opposition to the dignity both of human procreation and of the conjugal union.*
>
> (*Donum Vitae* 1.6)

e) Revealed ethics

Many Christians who may not support natural law do nevertheless consider that there is a natural order to the creation as revealed in Genesis 1. Genesis 1 suggests that there are 'orders of creation' which have been given their place by God which humans, as God's **stewards** on earth (Genesis 1:28), are to maintain. Cloning sets up humans in direct opposition to God as it places the origins of human life under the absolute control of humans rather than in the randomness of natural sexual procreation.

- **Marriage**. Asexual procreation cannot be accepted within any Christian tradition which considers the female/male bond in marriage to correspond to the God/world relationship. The process of creating life is not just a biological one but one which requires the intimacy and love of two individuals to create another human being who is also loved and wanted. Cloning confuses and destroys this intimate relationship by eliminating the need for two parents and their gift of love to each other which may result in the gift of a child.
- **Families**. Could a cloned person become part of a happy family? Traditional Christianity does not regard a child as a right but as a gift of creation. Reproductive cloning removes the sense that a person belongs to and is a result of a complex set of loving relationships. The image conveyed in the New Testament is that the family is the 'body of Christ' (Ephesians 5:29) ordered and guided in relationship with Christ, at the heart of which is marriage and sexual reproduction (Ephesians 5:30).

On the other hand many Christians feel that sometimes too much is made of the physical aspects of relationships. Families are made up of more than biological affinity and are based on love, friendship and companionship. A cloned person could be part of a family as anyone else. Even though their genetic relationship to their donor is unusual, that is not sufficient reason to reject it as being necessarily wrong. As we have seen, there are many liberal Christians who see in nature vast potentials which have yet to be fully realised. St Paul described nature as 'groaning' and yearning for completion. Nature is not static but has more to offer us; science and technology, as Ian Barbour argued above, make this a possibility providing this is done in partnership with God.

> *because the creation itself will be set free from bondage to decay and obtain the glorious liberty of the children of God. We know that the whole creation has been groaning in travail together until now.*
>
> (Romans 8:21–22)

But others, whilst seeing the potential of technology, are less certain. In its report *Personal Origins* (1996), the Church of England concluded that because human persons are both body and spirit there are limits set by the spirit as to how far the body can be subject to technical manipulation. Even if creation is open-ended and in the process of completion, Christianity teaches that there are limits to how we should treat the body. That is why sexual immorality and suicide, for example, are both seen as abuses of the body. Cloning threatens to cheapen the spiritual aspect of the body by treating it as a thing to be manipulated or even destroyed (through the creation of embryonic stem (ES) cells). Finally, if technology comes to symbolise **dominion** over ourselves, then cloning especially suggests that we also have the power to dominate others. If this is so, then it would be contrary to Jesus' teaching on the Kingdom of God as a state of generosity, protection of the weak and of justice:

> *personal dominion over ourselves threatens to become dominion of some people over other people. The covenant we make with one with another, our equality before God and within the community of fellowship, may be threatened if we view one another only as a body which may be used for whatever good purpose we choose. The existence of codes of ethics (such as the Hippocratic Oath and the Helsinki Declaration) governing scientific experiments on human subjects is clear acknowledgement of this. Indeed we can learn from the limits imposed by these codes.*
>
> (*Personal Origins*, page 30)

Summary diagram

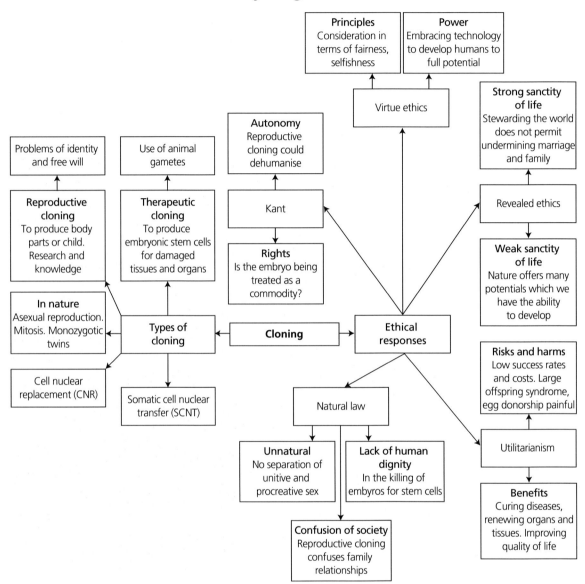

Study guide

By the end of this chapter, you should have considered why scientists would want to clone humans and the differences in aims between therapeutic and reproductive cloning. You should be able to assess how much of this is a present reality and how much exaggerated claims. You should also have considered the problem of scientific knowledge and how it should be used. You should have considered the implications of reproductive cloning for human free will and authentic human existence. In conclusion you should have considered the various normative ethical systems and assessed those who are pessimistic and repelled by cloning as well as those who are optimistic about its future.

Revision checklist

Can you define the following:

- reproductive and therapeutic cloning
- asexual reproduction
- monozygotic twins
- CNR, SCNT and embryonic splitting.

Can you state:

- three risks of therapeutic cloning
- three risks of reproductive cloning
- the law on therapeutic and reproductive cloning
- the aim of the Human Genome Project.

Can you explain:

- why some are pessimistic and some are optimistic about cloning technology
- Leon Kass' 'wisdom of repugnancy' and its purpose
- why a cloned human being may or may not be a defective human person
- Kantian arguments on the treatment of clones for body parts
- revealed ethical arguments on cloning in terms of family relationships and the body–spirit relationship.

Can you give the arguments for and against:

- the creation of chimeras and hybrids
- cloning in terms of eugenics and use of resources
- cloning in terms of Nietzsche's will to power
- cloning in terms of being stewards (or co-workers) of nature.

Essay question

1. Assess the view that human cloning undermines human dignity.

Demonstration of knowledge and understanding might involve explaining that the ethical issues vary depending whether cloning refers to therapeutic or reproductive purposes. A brief definition of the two aims of cloning will be necessary. A general pessimistic response might begin with Tong's 'genomic trap' view and develop this further through Kant's and Sartre's views that a cloned human might feel less authentic than other humans. Therapeutic cloning might begin with the natural law rejection of any method which has to destroy the embryo for stem cells or cannibalised for tissue or organ parts. Optimistic views might focus on those who see the potential of nature and like Nietzsche consider that the benefits of cloning are worth taking the risks. The utilitarian position is useful to weigh up what these risks might be.

Evaluation may focus on discussion of reproductive cloning. It might be helpful to make an assessment of different theories of free will and determinism and to consider what exactly is meant by 'human dignity'. Kass' 'repugnancy' notion might be discussed here and assessed in terms of its rational basis, perhaps with reference to Kant. Conclusions might distinguish between therapeutic and reproductive cloning, or consider both to be the same.

Further essay questions

2a   Explain the reasons for reproductive human cloning.

2b   Discuss the view that even though the results of human cloning are uncertain we should risk developing it.

3a   Explain the reasons for therapeutic human cloning.

3b   Assess the view that human cloning is against natural law.

4   'Human cloning offers humans enormous benefits.' Discuss.

GLOSSARY

abrogation to defy a rule, duty or law and therefore to abolish.

altruism a free and generous act for others.

amniocentesis when a small amount of amniotic fluid is taken from the womb. It contains foetal DNA which can be tested. It can cause harm to the foetus.

antinomianism no laws or rules.

begging the question when the conclusion is contained in one of the premises of the question.

Cartesian the adjective describing those who follow Descartes' view of the soul.

chimera an organism containing a mixture of different genetic tissues which originated from different zygotes or the fusing together of early embryos.

commodification to treat the body as an object which can be bought and sold.

dead donor rule based on the same principle which also forbids euthanasia. It is wrong for doctors deliberately to end a patient's life for whatever reason.

deontology the belief that there are duties or rules that are intrinsically right.

dialysis the process by which a machine can perform the task of the defective organ (usually a kidney).

dualists mind–body dualists believe that souls and bodies are made of quite different substances.

ectopic pregnancy where the foetus is developing in the fallopian tubes, not in the uterus. This usually proves fatal to mother and baby.

empirical gaining knowledge through observation and experience rather than logic or theory.

epistemology the study of knowledge.

eugenics comes from the Greek meaning 'well born'. The term eugenics has been used to refer to the process of selective breeding with the aim of improving society.

gamete a sex cell (i.e. egg or sperm) containing half the number of chromosomes (i.e. 23 for humans) and capable of fusing with a gamete of the opposite sex to produce a fertilised egg.

genome a complete set of genetic information.

heterozygous when the adult has both the disease-causing recessive gene and the normal dominant gene. They do not show symptoms of the disease but have the potential, as a carrier, to pass on the gene to their offspring.

holiness 'set apart' or sanctified. It is this word which gives rise to the phrase 'sanctity of life'.

Human Fertilisation and Embryology Act of 1990 presently undergoing a major revision. The new Act under the same name is due for royal consent in 2008.

hybrid created by cross-breeding different animals.

if and only if if and only if... statements are the usual way of expressing necessary and sufficient conditions.

incarnation the Christian notion that God became human in the form of Jesus Christ.

infinite regress where each idea implies a preceding idea without an origin. If this is so there is no reason to accept any one idea as being any more true than any other.

instrumental value an action is good by what it achieves.

licit (lawful) and **illicit** (unlawful) important terms in natural law.

liver transplants live donor transplants began in 1987 and consist of taking a liver lobe from the donor and transplanting it in the recipient. The lobe should grow back.

mandatory compulsory under law.

maxim Kant defines maxim as a 'subjective principle of acting' that is a general rule or principle governing the action of all rational people.

mitochondria found in the cytoplasm (the area outside the nucleus) of the ovum. They are the site of aerobic respiration which releases energy for the cell to develop.

monozygotic twins twins who are genetically almost identical as they have developed from the same egg and sperm.

naprotechnology or **natural procreative technology** a women's health science that monitors and maintains a woman's reproductive and gynaecological health. It provides medical and surgical treatments which work naturally with her reproductive system.

natural law everything has its purpose or *telos*. Aquinas suggested that humans have five related primary ends. The spiritual *telos* is the worship of God.

non-maleficence one of the four basic principles of doctors' ethics (the others being autonomy, beneficence and justice).

ontological the discussion or description of how something actually exists.

palliative giving pain-relieving care.

parental order equivalent to adoption but quicker. It can be obtained by applying to the courts.

pre-embryo describes the embryo from conception to 14 days old.

primitive streak later forms the spinal cord.

Promethean using human intelligence to further our own existence. The idea is based on the Greek myth where Prometheus stole fire from Zeus for humans to use.

psychosomatic literally spirit–body. The soul or spirit is the life-principle of the body.

slavery when a person is owned by another as their property. As property they can be sold and traded to another person. Slavery is against Article 4 of the Universal Declaration of Human Rights, 'No one shall be held in slavery or servitude; slavery and the slave trade shall be prohibited in all their forms.'

somatic cells these are not sex cells and contain a full set of genes. The adult nucleus has to be 'switched off' so that it ceases to behave in its specialised way. Reproductive cells refer to sperm and ova.

stem cells undifferentiated somatic cells which are capable of either division to give rise to daughter stem cells or, when given the appropriate signal, can become any specialised cell type. They can be found in bone marrow, growing tissues, and embryonic tissue.

sufficient reason the principle developed by Leibnitz which states that for every fact there must be a reason why it is so.

surrogacy when a woman bears a child for another woman or couple.

totipotent 'having unlimited capability'. The term pluripotent is also used to mean 'having many capabilities'.

transplantation removing an organ and replanting it or re-establishing it in someone else.

unitive this aspect to sexual intercourse describes both the physical act itself and the psychological dimension of love.

vices vices described by Aristotle are either deficient or excessive application of virtue. For example the vices of modesty are shyness and shamelessness.

vitalism the view that for the human body to be alive it must also possess a soul.

weak sanctity of life by using the term 'weak' the sanctity of life principle is modified to allow for exceptions, e.g. human life should not always be preserved at all costs.

xenotransplantation cross-animal organ transfer.

FURTHER READING

Agar, Nicholas, *Perfect Copy* (Icon Books, 2002)

Aristotle, *Ethics*, Book 2 (Translated by JAK Thomson. Penguin, 1976)

Barbour, Ian, *Nature, Human Nature and God* (SPCK, 2002)

Beauchamp, Tom and Childress, James, *Principles of Biomedical Ethics* (OUP, 1994, 4th edition)

Bentham, Jeremy, *An Introduction to the Principles of Morals and Legislation* (Dover Publications, 2007)

BMA, *The Handbook of Medical Ethics* (BMA, 1986)

Campbell, Alastair and Higgs, Roger, *In That Case: Medical Ethics in Everyday Practice* (Darton, Longman and Todd, 1982)

Catholic Church, *Catechism of the Catholic Church* (Geoffrey Chapman, 1994)

Charlesworth, Max, *Bioethics in a Liberal Society* (CUP, 1993)

Church of England, *Personal Origins* (Church House Publishing, 1996, 2nd edition)

Dyson, Anthony, *The Ethics of IVF* (Mowbray, 1995)

Fletcher, Joseph, *Situation Ethics* (Westminster John Knox Press, 1966)

Fletcher, Joseph, *Humanhood: Essays in Biomedical Ethics* (Prometheus Books, 1979)

Fulford, KWM *et al.*, *Medicine and Moral Reasoning* (CUP, 1994)

Glover, Jonathan, *Causing Death and Saving Lives* (Penguin, 1990)

Harris, John, *The Value of Life: Introduction to Medical Ethics* (Routledge, 1985)

Hauerwas, Stanley, *Suffering Presence: Theological Reflections on Medicine, the Mentally Handicapped, and the Church* (T & T Clark, 1988)

Hope, Tony, *Medical Ethics: A Very Short Introduction* (OUP, 2004)

Hope, Tony, Savulescu, Julian and Hendrick, Judith, *Medical Ethics and Law: The Core Curriculum* (Churchill Livingstone, 2008, 2nd edition)

John Paul II, *Evangelium Vitae* (Catholic Truth Society, 1995)

Jones, David Albert, *Organ Transplants and the Definition of Death* (CTS, 2001)

Jones, David Albert, *The Soul of the Embryo* (Continuum, 2004)

Linzey, Andrew, *Animal Theology* (SCM, 1994)

McCarthy, Anthony, *Cloning* (Catholic Truth Society, 2003)

Messer, Neil, *Christian Ethics* (SCM, 2006)

Mill, John Stuart, *Utilitarianism* (edited by Mary Warnock) (Collins, 1962)

Overall, Christine, *Human Reproduction: Principles, Practices and Policies* (OUP, 1993)

Pence, Gregory, *Classic Cases in Medical Ethics* (McGraw Hill, 2007)

Ramsey, Paul, *Fabricated Man* (Yale University Press, 1970)

Sartre, Jean-Paul, *Existentialism and Humanism* (Methuen, 1973)

Singer, Peter (ed.), *Applied Ethics* (OUP, 1986)

Singer, Peter (ed.), *Embryo Experimentation: Ethical, Legal and Social Issues* (CUP, 1990)

Singer, Peter (ed.), *A Companion to Ethics* (Blackwell, 1993)

Singer, Peter, *Practical Ethics* (CUP, 1993)

Singer, Peter, *Rethinking Life and Death: The Collapse of Our Traditional Ethics* (OUP, 1995)

Smart, JCC and Williams, Bernard, *Utilitarianism: For and Against* (CUP, 1973)

Steinbock, Bonnie (ed.), *The Oxford Handbook of Bioethics* (OUP, 2007)

Sutton, Agneta, *Infertility* (CTS, 2003)

Thompson, Mel, *Ethical Theory* (Hodder, 2008, 3rd edition)

Tong, Rosemary, *Feminist Approaches to Bioethics* (Westview Press, 1997)

Warnock, Mary, *A Question of Life* (Blackwell, 1985)

Watt, Helen, *Life and Death in Healthcare Ethics* (Routledge, 2000)

Watt, Helen, *Gene Therapy and Human Genetic Engineering* (CTS, 2003)

Wilcockson, Michael, *Issues of Life and Death* (Hodder, 2008, 2nd edition)

On-line resources for this book and others in the series

New books and websites are appearing all the time.
Keep up-to-date and share your own suggestions with other students and teachers.

For suggestions for further reading, comments from the authors of the *Access to Religion and Philosophy* series and further advice for students and teachers, **log on to the** *Access to Religion and Philosophy* **website at:**

www.philosophyandethics.com/access.htm

INDEX